Thinking Critically:
E-cigarettes and Vaping

Christine Wilcox

ReferencePoint
Press®

San Diego, CA

Picture Credits:
9: Mauro Grigollo/iStockphoto.com;
15, 22, 29, 34, 41, 45, 52, 58: Maury Aaseng

LIBRARY OF CONGRESS CATALOGING-IN-PUBLICATION DATA

Names: Wilcox, Christine, author.
Title: E-cigarettes and vaping / by Christine Wilcox.
Description: San Diego, CA : ReferencePoint Press, 2016. | Series: Thinking critically | Includes bibliographical references and index.
Identifiers: LCCN 2015034207| ISBN 9781601529565 (hardback) | ISBN 1601529562 (hardback)
Subjects: LCSH: Smoking--Juvenile literature. | Electronic cigarettes--Juvenile literature. | Teenagers--Tobacco use--Juvenile literature.
Classification: LCC HV5745 .W54 2016 | DDC 362.29/6--dc23 LC record available at http://lccn.loc.gov/2015034207

Contents

Foreword

"Literacy is the most basic currency of the knowledge economy we're living in today." Barack Obama (at the time a senator from Illinois) spoke these words during a 2005 speech before the American Library Association. One question raised by this statement is: What does it mean to be a literate person in the twenty-first century?

E.D. Hirsch Jr., author of *Cultural Literacy: What Every American Needs to Know*, answers the question this way: "To be culturally literate is to possess the basic information needed to thrive in the modern world. The breadth of the information is great, extending over the major domains of human activity from sports to science."

But literacy in the twenty-first century goes beyond the accumulation of knowledge gained through study and experience and expanded over time. Now more than ever literacy requires the ability to sift through and evaluate vast amounts of information and, as the authors of the Common Core State Standards state, to "demonstrate the cogent reasoning and use of evidence that is essential to both private deliberation and responsible citizenship in a democratic republic."

The *Thinking Critically* series challenges students to become discerning readers, to think independently, and to engage and develop their skills as critical thinkers. Through a narrative-driven, pro/con format, the series introduces students to the complex issues that dominate public discourse—topics such as gun control and violence, social networking, and medical marijuana. All chapters revolve around a single, pointed question such as Can Stronger Gun Control Measures Prevent Mass Shootings?, or Does Social Networking Benefit Society?, or Should Medical Marijuana Be Legalized? This inquiry-based approach introduces student researchers to core issues and concerns on a given topic. Each chapter includes one part that argues the affirmative and one part that argues the negative—all written by a single author. With the single-author format the predominant arguments for and against an issue can be synthesized into clear, accessible discussions supported by details and evidence including relevant facts, direct quotes, current examples, and statistical illustrations. All volumes include focus questions to guide students as they read each pro/con discussion, a list of key facts, and an annotated list of related organizations and websites for conducting further research.

The authors of the Common Core State Standards have set out the particular qualities that a literate person in the twenty-first century must have. These include the ability to think independently, establish a base of knowledge across a wide range of subjects, engage in open-minded but discerning reading and listening, know how to use and evaluate evidence, and appreciate and understand diverse perspectives. The new *Thinking Critically* series supports these goals by providing a solid introduction to the study of pro/con issues.

Overview

E-cigarettes and Vaping

E-cigarettes were introduced to the US market in 2007. Since that time, vaping—inhaling the nicotine-laced vapor created by electronic smoking devices, or ESDs—has exploded in popularity, especially among young people. ESDs are credited with helping people quit smoking, which has the potential to prevent the millions of deaths caused by cigarette smoking each year worldwide. However, the devices have come under attack from anti-tobacco groups, which claim that ESDs have adverse health consequences and encourage nonsmoking young people to use tobacco products.

What Are ESDs?

ESDs are battery-powered devices that heat a liquid until it turns into an aerosol—a gas that has tiny droplets of liquid suspended in it. There are many types of ESDs, and the products go by many different names. Cig-a-likes are ESDs that are made to resemble cigarettes. Popular brands like blu and NJOY—both manufactured by tobacco companies—can be found in stores that sell tobacco products. Vape pens, which are about the size of a magic marker or cigar, deliver more vapor than cig-a-likes and are refillable. APVs (advanced personal vaporizers), or mods, are about the size of a small flashlight (tube mod) or a pack of cigarettes (box mod); they have replaceable batteries and other upgrades such as variable heat settings and digital readouts. APVs are mainly used by experienced vapers (people who vape) who want the maximum amount of vapor in each inhalation. All of these devices tend to be referred to as *e-cigarettes* by the media for convenience, though vapers usually use the term *e-cigarette* to refer to cig-a-likes. ESDs also go by the name *electronic nicotine delivery systems,* or *ENDS.* However, since some people enjoy vaping e-liquid with zero nicotine, the acronym *ESD* is more accurate.

The liquid that is vaporized in an ESD is called e-liquid. E-liquid is usually made up of four ingredients: propylene glycol, vegetable glycerin, liquid nicotine, and food-grade flavorings. Propylene glycol and vegetable glycerin are used in many food products, and both produce a smoky vapor when heated. Nicotine is a naturally occurring insecticide produced by plants in the nightshade family, such as the tobacco plant. When smoked or vaporized, nicotine acts as both a stimulant and a depressant—in small doses it makes the user feel alert; in slightly larger doses it has a calming effect. Nicotine is highly addictive, but inhaling nicotine is relatively harmless and may have some health benefits. However, when ingested or absorbed through the skin in large doses, liquid nicotine is toxic. Consumers can usually customize the amount of nicotine, propylene glycol, glycerin, and flavorings in their e-liquid.

There is little scientific research on the health effects of ESDs and e-liquids, and virtually no long-term studies. The studies that have been done often contradict each other. Some show that ESD vapor contains cancer-causing contaminants and that propylene glycol can irritate lung tissue and make people more susceptible to lung infections. Other studies show that these health risks are minimal and on par with risks associated with stop-smoking aids like nicotine patches. The risks from secondhand vapor are also unclear—some studies show the vapor contains contaminants and nicotine, whereas others show that levels of these substances are so low that the risk is negligible. In addition, while the flavorings added to e-liquids are safe to eat, they may not be safe to inhale.

> **"What's most surprising is how incredibly rapidly the use of [ESD] products other than cigarettes have increased."[1]**
>
> —Dr. Tom Frieden, director of the CDC.

Prevalence

The percentage of adults who have used ESDs at least once almost tripled from 2010 to 2013, rising from 3.3 percent to 8.5 percent. Use by adolescents also increased threefold. The National Youth Tobacco Survey, published in April 2015 by the Centers for Disease Control and Prevention (CDC), found that 13.4 percent of high school students had used an ESD in the month before the survey, up from 4.5 percent in 2013. Use by middle school students also increased to 3.9 percent from 1.1 percent in 2013. As Dr. Tom Frieden, director of the CDC, notes, "What's most surprising is how incredibly rapidly the use of [ESD] products other than cigarettes have increased."[1]

These increases—especially among adolescents—have prompted concern among lawmakers and antismoking advocates that ESDs may addict nonsmoking young people to nicotine and lead to tobacco use. However, despite these concerns, teen smoking has steadily declined. The National Youth Tobacco Survey revealed that 9.2 percent of high school students had used cigarettes in the past month, down from 12.7 percent in 2013—a drop of about 25 percent. Smoking among middle school students stayed about the same; 2.5 percent reported past-month cigarette use, down from 2.9 percent in 2013.

> "[E-liquids] come in kid-friendly flavors, including chocolate, bubble gum and gummy bear."[2]
>
> —Dina Fine Maron, editor for health and medicine, *Scientific American*.

Controversy

Even though scientific research about ESDs is still in its infancy, almost everyone agrees that ESDs are far less dangerous than cigarettes. Because of this, the controversy over ESDs centers on which is more important: to encourage smokers to switch to ESDs or to discourage young people from using these products.

Anti-vaping activists claim that ESDs are a gateway to cigarette smoking—addicting nonsmoking young people to nicotine and encouraging them to try tobacco products. These activists are also concerned that the popularity of vaping undermines the social stigma against cigarette smoking, which also encourages young people to smoke. In addition, they say that the ESD industry is targeting young people—both in

Electronic smoking devices, including e-cigarettes and vape pens, are gaining in popularity among both adults and teens. Although few scientific studies have been done on the health effects of ESDs, support for increased government regulation has been mounting.

its advertising and by creating sweet flavors that appeal to kids. As Dina Fine Maron writes in *Scientific American,* "They come in kid-friendly flavors, including chocolate, bubble gum and gummy bear."[2] These activists believe that the best way to protect children from ESDs is to regulate them like other tobacco products.

Pro-vaping activists are concerned that regulating ESDs like tobacco products will discourage smokers from switching to ESDs. They claim that ESDs are an effective stop-smoking aid, and because they are much less dangerous than smoking, ESDs have the potential to save the millions of lives lost each year to lung cancer, emphysema, and other diseases caused by cigarette smoke. If ESDs become harder for adults to obtain, if they are banned in public spaces, or if sweet flavors are eliminated, fewer smokers will quit smoking and fewer lives will be saved, activists say.

Regulation

When ESDs came on the market in 2007, they were not classified as food products, nicotine delivery devices, or tobacco products. As such, they were unregulated on the federal level. Manufacturers were not required to list ingredients, use safe manufacturing practices, or issue warnings about the potential dangers of these products. And even though almost all ESD manufacturers support a ban on sales to young people, there was no federal ban on sales to minors. Because of this lack of federal regulation, states began passing laws restricting ESD use. Over forty states have issued bans on sales of ESDs and e-liquids to minors, and many have gone further, such as banning vaping in places where smoking is banned and requiring Internet sales sites to use age-verification software.

In April 2014 the US Food and Drug Administration (FDA) announced that it would regulate ESDs and e-liquids as tobacco products. The rules it proposed would ban the sale of ESDs and e-liquids to anyone under eighteen, prohibit vaping in areas where smoking is not allowed by law, ban free samples, require warning labels and childproof safety caps on all e-liquids, restrict advertising, and ban most sweet flavorings because of their appeal to children. ESDs and e-liquids would also be required to undergo premarket government review. Manufacturers would be required to provide the FDA with a detailed list of ingredients for each product, describe the manufacturing process, submit to inspections, and provide scientific data about safety.

According to the *Wall Street Journal*, the premarket review process would cost manufacturers $2 million to $10 million per product. In the case of e-liquid manufacturers, each individual flavor is considered a product. In addition, rules may retroactively apply to all products that entered the market after 2007, which means that ESDs and e-liquids on the market now could not be sold until they were approved. Most industry experts say that if these rules are put in place, the only companies that will be able to meet the financial burden will be big tobacco companies that manufacture cig-a-likes, and that thousands of small and medium-sized ESD businesses will close.

The Future of E-cigarettes

As of September 2015, the FDA had not yet issued any federal regulations concerning ESDs. Experts said that the agency was weighing the health benefits to smokers who switch to ESDs against the possible gateway effect on young people. Many in the ESD industry hoped that regulation would do both—promote ESD use by smokers while discouraging its use by young people. "I think that regulation is not a bad thing," says Shadi Khoury, the owner of Indy E-cigs in Indiana. "I think over-intrusive regulation is the problem."[3] Whether regulations will be able to achieve this balance remains to be seen.

Chapter One

Are E-cigarettes and Vaping a Health Hazard?

E-cigarettes and Vaping Are a Health Hazard

- E-cigarettes have been shown to irritate lung tissue.
- E-cigarettes produce formaldehyde and other dangerous contaminants.
- Vaporized flavorings may be toxic.
- Nicotine can affect how the brain develops in children and teenagers.

The Debate at a Glance

E-cigarettes and Vaping Are Not a Health Hazard

- There is no proof that e-cigarettes pose a significant health risk.
- E-cigarettes are much safer than tobacco cigarettes.
- The ingredients in e-liquid are used in food and proven to be safe.
- Studies show that nicotine actually improves brain performance and protects against diseases like Parkinson's disease.

E-cigarettes and Vaping Are a Health Hazard

"E-cigarettes are definitely not benign."

—Dr. Laura Crotty Alexander is a pulmonary and critical care physician with the VA San Diego Healthcare System.

Quoted in Janet Raloff, "Health Risks of E-cigarettes Emerge," *ScienceNews*, June 3, 2014. www.science news.org.

Consider these questions as you read:

1. How persuasive is the argument that e-cigarettes and vaping should not be considered a safe alternative to smoking tobacco cigarettes? Explain your answer.
2. One scientist argues that teens who try nicotine-containing products like ESDs are "playing Russian roulette with the brain." Do you think this analogy is supported by evidence? Why or why not?
3. Do you think the reported side effects of vaping are acceptable if vaping helps a person quit smoking tobacco products? Explain your answer.

Editor's note: The discussion that follows presents common arguments made in support of this perspective, reinforced by facts, quotes, and examples taken from various sources.

E-cigarette and vaping advocates claim that ESDs do not damage health and that e-liquids contain only ingredients that are proven to be safe. However, most of the ingredients in e-liquids have not been tested in vapor form, and their effects on the lungs are just becoming known. Initial studies have found that these ingredients can irritate and damage lung tissue. According to Dr. Cathy McDonald, who runs a tobacco-dependence treatment program in Alameda County, California, "Ten minutes after smoking an e-cigarette—for a person who has never smoked a cigarette—

. . . [there is] a noticeable increase in airway resistance in the lungs."[4] Because of these side effects, ESDs should be considered hazardous to respiratory health and should not be considered a safe alternative to smoking.

ESDs Damage Lung Tissue

While research is ongoing, initial experiments have found that the main ingredient in most e-liquids—propylene glycol—irritates lung tissue. Propylene glycol is a form of mineral oil found in many household products, including antifreeze, solvents, flavors and fragrances, cosmetics, plastics, and many food products. Although it is considered safe to eat, according to its product safety information, inhalation of "mist may cause irritation of upper respiratory tract" and "in rare cases, repeated exposure to propylene glycol may cause central nervous system effects."[5]

> "Ten minutes after smoking an e-cigarette . . . [there is] a noticeable increase in airway resistance in the lungs."[4]
>
> —Dr. Cathy McDonald, who runs a tobacco-dependence treatment program in Alameda County, California.

The adverse effects of propylene glycol were first described among theater actors and crew members who worked near theater fog machines, which create vapor by heating propylene glycol in much the same way an ESD does. The constant exposure to the vapor caused coughing, dry throat, headaches, dizziness, chest tightness, wheezing, and reduced lung function.

Studies have confirmed that propylene glycol can damage lung tissue. A 2015 article in the *American Journal of Medicine* reports that significant exposure to propylene glycol mist "can cause irritation of the upper and lower respiratory track mucosa." In addition, e-cigarette vapor has been linked to bronchial infections and pneumonia. According to the article, "Although uncommon, these cases point to the unpredictable and potential serious side effects of e-cigarettes."[6]

ESDs Produce Formaldehyde

Another danger of using ESDs is that many of them produce formaldehyde. Formaldehyde is a colorless gas used in embalming fluid that has

Teen Brains Especially Vulnerable to Nicotine Addiction

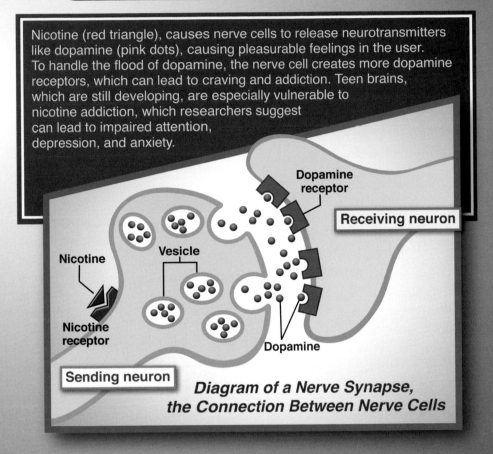

Nicotine (red triangle), causes nerve cells to release neurotransmitters like dopamine (pink dots), causing pleasurable feelings in the user. To handle the flood of dopamine, the nerve cell creates more dopamine receptors, which can lead to craving and addiction. Teen brains, which are still developing, are especially vulnerable to nicotine addiction, which researchers suggest can lead to impaired attention, depression, and anxiety.

Dopamine receptor

Receiving neuron

Nicotine

Vesicle

Nicotine receptor

Dopamine

Sending neuron

Diagram of a Nerve Synapse, the Connection Between Nerve Cells

Source: Janet Raloff, "E-cigarettes Proving to Be a Danger to Teens," *ScienceNews*, June 30, 2015. www.sciencenews.org.

been shown to cause cancer in laboratory animals and has been linked to some human cancers, including throat and nasal cancers and leukemia. The gas is formed as a by-product of some chemical reactions, including the heating of propylene glycol and glycerin—the two main ingredients of e-liquid.

A 2015 study in the *New England Journal of Medicine* found that some ESDs may produce five to fifteen times more formaldehyde than tobacco cigarettes. This is more likely to occur in newer ESDs that have very hot heating devices—which can burn hotter than 1,000°F (538°C). "When [e-liquid] gets really hot, unwanted reactions occur,"[7] explains James Pankow, professor of chemistry and engineering at Portland State University in Oregon and one of the study's authors. The study estimates that vaping 3 milligrams of e-liquid at a high temperature can create 14 milligrams of formaldehyde—compared to the roughly 3 milligrams that is typically created by smoking an entire pack of cigarettes. This estimate "may be conservative,"[8] Pankow says.

> "These chemicals haven't been proven safe for inhalation."[10]
>
> —James Pankow, professor of chemistry and engineering at Portland State University in Oregon, on the flavor chemicals in e-liquids.

Formaldehyde is not the only dangerous substance produced by ESDs. In January 2015 the California Department of Public Health issued a report that stated e-cigarette vapor contains at least ten chemicals that cause cancer or birth defects. ESD vapor also can contain tiny particles that are deposited deep in the lungs and may cause or worsen illnesses like asthma or bronchitis. "When they [the particles] deposit in your lungs, it makes it easy for whatever chemicals are in them to dissolve into your lung tissue,"[9] explains Jonathan Thornburg, who led a study on e-cigarette vapor at the research institute RTI International in North Carolina.

Flavorings May Not Be Safe

One of the biggest concerns about the effects of ESDs is the safety of the hundreds of different food-grade flavorings used in e-liquids. Although these flavorings have long been found to be safe for human consumption, the effects of inhaling them in vapor are largely unknown. "I think the e-cigarette folks are kind of in a bit of a box," said Pankow. "First of all, they are saying they're using food-grade chemicals. But they're not really safe, because these chemicals haven't been proven safe for inhalation."[10]

Several common flavor chemicals have already been associated with health problems. In 2015 Pankow coauthored a second study on the dangers of e-liquid flavorings. The study, published in *Tobacco Control*, notes that two common flavorings—vanillin and benzaldehyde—have been shown to irritate the respiratory tract, much like smog. The authors found double the amount of vanillin and benzaldehyde in e-cigarette vapor than is considered safe for workplace exposure. They concluded: "The concentrations of some flavour chemicals in e-cigarette fluids are sufficiently high for inhalation exposure by vaping to be of toxicological concern."[11]

Another flavoring, diacetyl, has been linked to a disease called bronchiolitis obliterans, also known as popcorn workers' lung. It was first described among workers at a microwave popcorn plant, which used the flavoring to give popcorn its buttery flavor. People suffering from popcorn lung have inflammation and scarring in the lungs' airways, which can cause severe shortness of breath and can be life threatening.

Nicotine Harms Teen Brains

Finally, nicotine itself can have adverse consequences on brain function—especially in teenagers. A 2011 study at the University of California–Los Angeles asked twenty-five smokers and nonsmokers between ages fifteen and twenty-one to do a task that involved the prefrontal cortex—the part of the brain involved in decision making and self-control. The study found that the greater a teen's addiction to nicotine, the less active the prefrontal cortex—suggesting that nicotine can affect brain function.

Teens also are much more vulnerable to nicotine addiction. According to Dr. Jonathan Winickoff from Harvard Medical School, "The most susceptible youth will lose autonomy over tobacco use after just a few times. So before they even know they're addicted, they'll first start wanting, then craving nicotine whenever they go too long between uses." This, Winickoff explains, is because the maturing brain will create more dopamine receptors in the presence of nicotine—which can lead to life-long addiction. "Essentially, this drug creates a biologic need that can be permanent," Winickoff says. "It also sets up the adolescent brain for more durable and stronger addiction pathways, not just for nicotine, but for other substances such as cocaine, marijuana and other drugs." He compares teens experimenting with e-cigarettes to "playing Russian roulette with the brain."[12]

Although experts are not suggesting that ESDs are as dangerous as cigarettes or other tobacco products, ESDs have been shown to harm healthy lung and respiratory function and in rare cases cause irreversible tissue damage. E-liquid manufacturers also use hundreds of different flavor chemicals—most of which have not been tested in aerosol form. The risk to health is substantial—especially among young people, who are more vulnerable to nicotine addiction and may develop lifelong smoking habits from using ESDs. Until scientists know more, ESDs should not be considered a safe alternative to smoking.

E-cigarettes and Vaping Are Not a Health Hazard

"The chemicals that they want you to be afraid of are the same chemicals that they say are okay for your food, toothpaste, shampoos, [and] medications."

—Jon Deak, CEO of Electronic Cigarette Consumer Reviews.

Jon Deak, "It's About Damn Time We Told the Truth About E-cigarettes!," Electronic Cigarette Consumer Reviews, January 29, 2015. www.electroniccigaretteconsumerreviews.com.

Consider these questions as you read:

1. How convincing is the argument that ESDs are safe? Explain your answer.
2. Do you think the researchers who claimed that ESD vapor contained high levels of formaldehyde should have been permitted to publish their study? Why or why not?
3. Do you think the media are to blame when e-cigarette users return to traditional tobacco products? Why or why not?

Editor's note: The discussion that follows presents common arguments made in support of this perspective, reinforced by facts, quotes, and examples taken from various sources.

Much has been made of the health hazards associated with e-cigarettes and vaping. Anti-vaping advocates note that ESD vapor contains known carcinogens, can cause lung irritation, and can lead to lifelong nicotine addiction. Unfortunately, the facts behind these claims are often taken out of context to give the impression that ESDs are inherently dangerous. But when compared to traditional tobacco cigarettes, ESDs are far safer and carry minimal risks. In fact, according to Peter Hajek, director of the Tobacco Dependence Research Unit at St. Bartholomew's

Hospital and the London School of Medicine and Dentistry, because of this relatively low risk to health, "smokers should be encouraged to switch to vaping."[13]

ESDs Much Safer than Cigarettes

Almost all health professionals agree that the long-term effects of ESD and e-liquids need to be studied. However, most scientists agree that ESDs are much less harmful to health than tobacco cigarettes. According to the American Lung Association, smoking-related diseases kill more than 393,000 Americans each year, and smoking "is the number one cause of preventable disease and death worldwide."[14] In comparison, ESD vapor has caused no deaths and has been associated only with minor health problems like throat and lung irritation. "E-cigarettes are new and we certainly don't yet have all the answers as to their long-term health impact," explains Ann McNeil, deputy director of the UK Centre for Tobacco and Alcohol Studies, "but what we do know is that they are much safer than cigarettes, which kill over 6 million people a year worldwide."[15]

> "What we do know is that [ESDs] are much safer than cigarettes."[15]
>
> —Ann McNeil, deputy director of the UK Centre for Tobacco and Alcohol Studies.

The reduced health risk of ESDs versus traditional cigarettes is important in that almost all vapers use or have used tobacco products. A 2015 survey of twelve hundred eleven- to sixteen-year-olds by Cancer Research UK found that only 2 percent used ESDs more than once a month and that only children who also smoked tobacco were regular ESD users. And a 2014 study published in *Tobacco Control* of ninety-three hundred adults in Minnesota found that 99 percent of the frequent vapers were also smokers. "Let's keep a sense of perspective here," says tobacco researcher and ESD advocate Dr. Michael Siegel. "Most of the individuals who are regular users of e-cigarettes are former smokers who have quit or current smokers. In either case, switching to vaping is the most important thing they can do to protect their health."[16]

This position has been supported by health organizations around the world. For instance, in its official statement about its position on e-cigarettes, the American Heart Association states that e-cigarettes contain fewer harmful ingredients than tobacco cigarettes and that smokers can lessen their health risk by switching to ESDs. And in the United Kingdom, both the National Institute for Health and Care Excellence and the Medicines & Healthcare Products Regulatory Association acknowledge that vaping is safer than smoking. "This is not simply an opinion, it is an evidence-based statement," states professor Linda Bauld about the organizations' positions. Bauld, who is deputy director of the UK Centre for Tobacco and Alcohol Studies, explains, "This does not mean e-cigarettes are risk free, but few things are. What it does mean is that their use is safer than continued smoking."[17]

One reason e-cigarettes are safer is that ESDs do not burn organic material like traditional cigarettes do. When tobacco is burned, particles of tar, hot gases, and other dangerous emissions are inhaled into the lungs, where they can lead to cancer, emphysema, and heart disease. What is vaporized are basic food ingredients used in asthma inhalers, such as propylene glycol and flavorings. Although these ingredients have not been proved to be completely safe to inhale, there have been no significant health issues reported by vapers since 2007, when ESDs entered the marketplace. According to Jon Deak, CEO of Electronic Cigarette Consumer Reviews, "It's not going to take an FDA chemist to tell us that 3 ingredients that are non-combustible are healthier than 4,000 dangerous carcinogenic chemicals in traditional cigarettes. . . . It's a no brainer!"[18]

Scientific Studies Not Reliable

The science surrounding ESDs and vaping is not always reliable. ESD advocates report that many of these studies are either flawed or are reported in a misleading fashion. For instance, a study by the American Chemical Society measured the amount of nicotine available for absorption in various samples of e-liquid. However, because most of the nicotine found was a type that is easily absorbed, the headline of the press release for the study proclaimed "E-cigarettes may be as addictive as traditional ones." According to ESD advocate Tom Pruen, "There is quite literally nothing in the

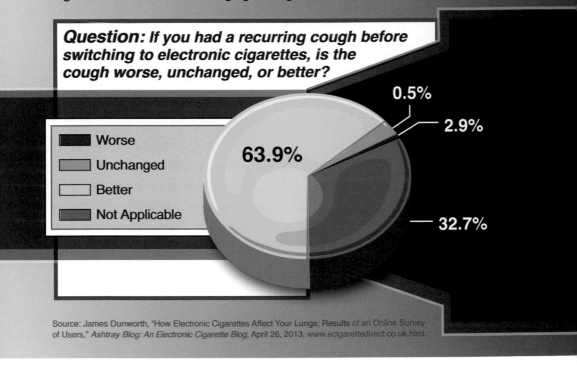

Switching to E-cigarettes Improves Smoker's Cough

A 2013 online survey of adults who vape found that almost two-thirds of them experienced an improvement of smoker's cough—the chronic cough sometimes suffered by tobacco smokers. In fact, of the 1,027 people who participated in the survey, only 5 reported that their smoker's cough worsened once they switched from cigarettes to e-cigarettes. The survey indicates that the vapor created by e-cigarettes is much less damaging to lung tissue than tobacco smoke.

Question: If you had a recurring cough before switching to electronic cigarettes, is the cough worse, unchanged, or better?

- Worse
- Unchanged
- Better
- Not Applicable

0.5%

2.9%

63.9%

32.7%

Source: James Dunworth, "How Electronic Cigarettes Affect Your Lungs: Results of an Online Survey of Users," *Ashtray Blog: An Electronic Cigarette Blog*, April 26, 2013. www.ecigarettedirect.co.uk.html.

study to support this headline." He notes that no comparisons were made between ESDs and traditional cigarettes and that addictive potential was not measured. "The press release . . . misrepresents the research that was done, and . . . appears to be intentionally dishonest." This is part of a larger trend that Pruen sees; he says it is common to see headlines that are "alarmist" and "scaremongering"[19] when it comes to the safety of ESDs.

Another study that has received a lot of attention in the media was published by the *New England Journal of Medicine* in January 2015. The study's title was "Hidden Formaldehyde in E-cigarette Aerosols," and it found that formaldehyde levels in some e-liquids were up to fifteen times higher than those in traditional cigarettes. However, another team of scientists debunked this study. The team pointed out that the original researchers overheated the ESDs, which resulted in "excessive breakdown of propylene glycol to formaldehyde. This phenomenon is readily detected by the consumer by virtue of an exceedingly unpleasant burning taste, commonly referred to as a 'dry puff.' . . . Thus, taste prevents e-cigarette users from exposing themselves to excessive formaldehyde from overheating of the coil."[20] In other words, formaldehyde is produced only at temperatures that make vaping unpleasant.

New York Times opinion columnist Joe Nocera notes, "There is not much doubt that studies like this have an impact on the public perception of e-cigarettes."[21] He says that headlines that exaggerate the risks of ESDs have resulted in a decrease in the percentage of smokers who believe ESDs are safe. A 2014 study published in the journal *Nicotine & Tobacco Research* found that this misperception may be driving some people back to tobacco cigarettes. Almost a third of the people surveyed in the study who had abandoned ESDs and returned to smoking said they did so because they were worried that vaping was dangerous.

Nicotine Protects the Brain

Experts are also concerned about the nicotine content of many e-liquids, which they say can contain toxic levels of the addictive substance. Although it is true that ingesting e-liquid can be toxic, when inhaled in smoke or vapor, it is safe. According to Jean-François Etter, a professor at the University of Geneva and an internationally recognized expert on ESDs, "The problem is combusted tobacco, not nicotine. At the dosage used by vapers or users of nicotine gums or patches, nicotine is not toxic. Long term vaping is not a public health problem; not any more than long term use of nicotine gums."[22]

In fact, studies have shown that nicotine has therapeutic properties. Florida's *Tampa Bay Times* reports that a study of Alzheimer's disease patients found that those who wore nicotine patches were able to concentrate and remember better than those who did not. Another study showed that older people who were experiencing bouts of memory loss were able to improve their cognitive function with nicotine. Dan Hurley, author of *Smarter: The New Science of Building Brain Power*, notes that not only does nicotine protect the brain by increasing calcium absorption and reducing levels of toxic free radicals in brain cells, it also may protect against brain diseases like Parkinson's. Nicotine, he writes in *Discover* magazine, "may prove to be a weirdly, improbably effective drug for relieving or preventing a variety of neurological disorders."[23]

> "Long term vaping is not a public health problem; not any more than long term use of nicotine gums."[22]
>
> —Jean-François Etter, an internationally recognized expert on ESDs.

Although ESDs and e-liquids may not be 100 percent safe, they are substantially safer than smoking tobacco cigarettes. Switching from smoking to vaping can also confer many health benefits, including a reduced cancer risk. The nicotine some e-liquids contain may even be beneficial to people who are suffering mental decline or other brain disorders. These health benefits clearly outweigh any risks inherent in ESD and vaping.

Chapter Two

Does the E-cigarette Industry Target Minors?

The E-cigarette Industry Targets Minors

- Cartoons, sex, and celebrity endorsements are all used in ESD advertising to appeal to children and teens.
- The ESD industry advertises in media that has a high percentage of young viewers.
- Many e-liquids come in fruit, candy, and dessert flavors, which appeal to children.

The Debate at a Glance

The E-cigarette Industry Does Not Target Minors

- The ESD industry targets smokers who want to quit, not children.
- The industry self-regulates in an effort to keep ESDs out of the hands of children.
- E-liquids come in sweet flavors to appeal to ex-smokers, who prefer the flavors to tobacco and say the flavors help them quit.

The E-cigarette Industry Targets Minors

"It's disturbing that [ESD] ads are aimed at young people and seek to re-glamorize the idea of smoking."

—Matthew Myers is president of the Campaign for Tobacco-Free Kids.

Quoted in Peter Galuszka, "From the Ashes," *Richmond (VA) Style Weekly,* February 11, 2014. www.style weekly.com.

Consider these questions as you read:

1. How persuasive is the argument that the e-cigarette industry targets minors? Explain your answer.
2. One argument made here is that sweet flavors are designed to appeal to young people. Do you agree? Why or why not?
3. Do commercials for ESDs make the products seem desirable to teenagers? Explain your answer.

Editor's note: The discussion that follows presents common arguments made in support of this perspective, reinforced by facts, quotes, and examples taken from various sources.

The ESD industry uses the same advertising techniques that were once used by big tobacco companies to appeal to children. Commercials emphasizing the "cool factor" of vaping have appeared on network and cable channels, and more and more kid-friendly flavors like cotton candy and Koko Puffs have been developed. This deliberate targeting of underage consumers threatens to create a new generation of young people addicted to nicotine—and who are at risk of switching to tobacco products.

Commercials Target Teens

According to Matthew Myers, president of the Campaign for Tobacco-Free Kids, "Like cigarette companies, e-cigarette makers claim they don't market to kids. But they're using the same themes and tactics tobacco companies have long used to market regular cigarettes to kids."[24] These tactics include associating a confident, sexy spokesperson with their product to make using ESDs seem desirable or cool. For instance, a popular advertisement for blu e-cigarettes features the entertainer Jenny McCarthy; another features actor Stephen Dorff. "Countless celebrities—like Leonardo DiCaprio, Kate Moss and Robert Pattinson—have been photographed vaping. Other stars have 'lit up' on television shows like *Saturday Night Live*," writes Randye Hoder, a concerned parent. "There are sports sponsorships, celebrity pitchmen and free samples handed out like candy at underground parties." Hoder believes that, among teenagers, these advertising techniques have already been successful in taking away the stigma of smoking that young people today have grown up with. "'Smoking,' at least in the form of vaping, is becoming cool again,"[25] says Hoder.

ESD manufacturers have also used cartoons and sex in advertisements. Use of cartoon characters, a practice banned for traditional cigarette manufacturers, appeared on the website for blu e-cigarettes, for instance. The site featured a cartoon character named Mr. Cool, which the Campaign for Tobacco-Free Kids claims was "reminiscent of the Joe Camel cartoon character that so effectively marketed cigarettes to kids in the 1990s."[26] Sex is also a tried-and-true method used to sell products to teenagers. A *Sports Illustrated* ad, also for blu, featured the torso of a slim woman in a bikini with the tagline "Slim. Charged. Ready to go." Vince Willmore with the Campaign for Tobacco-Free Kids says it is obvious whom the company is trying to reach. "It's going to appeal to teenage boys," he explains. Ads like these reglamorize smoking without disclosing the risks or dangers. "Kids may view them as something they can use that's not going to harm their health without realizing that they contain very addictive nicotine,"[27] Willmore says.

> "E-cigarette makers . . . [are] using the same themes and tactics tobacco companies have long used to market regular cigarettes to kids."[24]
>
> —Matthew Myers, president of the Campaign for Tobacco-Free Kids.

Advertisers Seek Out Young Viewers

As big tobacco companies entered the ESD market and expanded advertising to traditional media like television, they exposed many more young people to ESD advertising. A 2014 study published in *Pediatrics* tracked all ESD advertising that aired on more than one hundred network and cable channels. It found that roughly 24 million television viewers between ages twelve and twenty-four are being exposed to ESD advertising. The study found that the number of children between twelve and seventeen who are exposed to these ads rose more than 250 percent between 2011 and 2013 and more than 320 percent for young adults between eighteen and twenty-four.

> "There seems little doubt that the [ESD] makers will consider teenage children as a major market."[28]
>
> —Dr. Norman Edelman, senior medical advisor for the American Lung Association.

This increase cannot be explained by an overall increase in advertising. The ESD industry has been deliberately placing its ads in places that young people will see them. The *Pediatrics* study found that more than three-quarters of ads identified were airing on networks that have large youth viewership, such as Comedy Central, TV Land, and VH1. Dr. Norman Edelman, senior medical advisor for the American Lung Association, was not surprised by these findings. "There seems little doubt that the [ESD] makers will consider teenage children as a major market and will market to them, albeit indirectly by indicating that they are 'for adults.'"[28]

Sweet Flavors Designed to Appeal to Children

The sweet flavors used in e-liquids are yet another attempt to appeal to children and teenagers. According to Ron Chapman, director of the California Department of Public Health, "The availability of e-cigarettes in a variety of candy and fruit flavors such as cotton candy, gummy bear, chocolate mint and grape makes these products highly appealing to young children and teens."[29] He notes that in 2009 flavorings were banned from tobacco cigarettes (except for menthol) because of their appeal to children.

Youth Heavily Exposed to E-cigarette Advertising

A survey by Legacy, an antismoking group, found that from January through November 2013, teens and young adults were heavily exposed to TV and print ads for e-cigarettes. An estimated 29.3 million teens and young adults were exposed to TV ads and 32.2 million were exposed to print ads for e-cigarettes. TV ads aired on networks such as Comedy Central, ABC Family, E!, and MTV. A total of 179 print ads for e-cigarettes ran during this period in magazines such as *Entertainment Weekly*, *Men's Journal*, and *Rolling Stone*. The study suggests that young people are a target market for ESD companies.

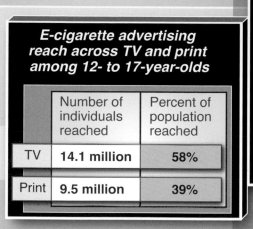

E-cigarette advertising reach across TV and print among 12- to 17-year-olds

	Number of individuals reached	Percent of population reached
TV	14.1 million	58%
Print	9.5 million	39%

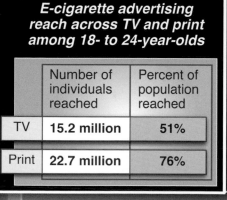

E-cigarette advertising reach across TV and print among 18- to 24-year-olds

	Number of individuals reached	Percent of population reached
TV	15.2 million	51%
Print	22.7 million	76%

Source: Center for Tobacco Control Research and Education, "Vaporized: E-cigarettes, Advertising, and Youth," May 2014. http://legacyforhealth.org.

Chapman and other critics want this rule expanded to include e-liquids. As Dr. David Kessler, former head of the FDA, and Myers write, "The 2009 law prohibited the sale of candy- and fruit-flavored cigarettes, and for good reason: Those cigarettes were a blatant appeal to teenagers. But e-cigarettes now come in more than 7,000 flavors. An extension of the flavored cigarette prohibition to e-cigarettes is more than justified. Adult e-cigarette users don't need flavors like cotton candy."[30]

Many teens do seem to prefer sweet flavors rather than tobacco or other flavors. "I like banana cream pie, because I like the sweetness, and it feels like you're eating or tasting the real thing,"[31] says fourteen-year-old Rebecca. "My favorite is gummy bears because it tastes really good,"[32] says Viviana, an eighth grader in the San Francisco Bay Area. Another eighth grader, Marleny, dislikes the smell and taste of burning tobacco. She says, "It has kind of a weird taste to it, like coffee without sugar."[33] She and most of her peers prefer dessert-inspired flavors. Clearly, many of these teens probably would not vape if only tobacco flavors were available.

The sweet flavors carry another danger—they make ESDs attractive to small children. Clouds of vapor produced by a dessert-flavored e-liquid smell sweet, and flavors like cotton candy and banana cream pie are easily recognizable by smell alone. This can lead to accidental overdoses by children drawn to the sweet-smelling liquid, and it can also encourage a small child to try his or her parent's ESD. Initial studies support this: A 2014 study published in Wales found that 6 percent of ten-year-olds had tried ESDs, whereas only 2 percent had tried tobacco.

Creating Lifelong Customers

Experts have said that the tobacco industry advertised cigarettes to children because they knew they would very likely create lifelong customers. Nicotine is extremely addictive; some have compared the difficulty in quitting to breaking a heroin addiction. It is even more addictive to children, whose brains are still developing. For this reason, ESD manufacturers should be forced to follow the same rules of advertising that apply to other nicotine-containing products like tobacco cigarettes—rules that protect children from addiction.

The E-cigarette Industry Does Not Target Minors

"Simply having flavors is not a marketing technique. That just means you're producing products that legal consumers are asking for."

—Alex Carlson is a pro-vaping advocate and creator of *Ridiculous! Vape Vlog.*

Alex Carlson, "NEW Study Shows Flavors Don't Appeal to Teens," Vaping Militia, January 9, 2015. http://thevapingmilitia.org.

Consider these questions as you read:

1. How convincing is the argument that the ESD industry does not target minors? Explain your answer.
2. Do you think the argument that smokers and teenagers have similar characteristics is accurate? Why or why not?
3. In your opinion, do you think kids would use ESDs if no sweet flavors were available? Explain.

Editor's note: The discussion that follows presents common arguments made in support of this perspective, reinforced by facts, quotes, and examples taken from various sources.

The ESD industry has been accused of deliberately targeting children in its advertising and product manufacturing. The industry denies this; it claims the customer it is targeting is the adult smoker and that celebrity ads and sweet e-liquids are designed to attract adults who want an enjoyable alternative to tobacco.

Adult Smokers Are the Target Consumer

Industry insiders deny that advertisements for ESDs are designed to appeal to children, teenagers, or even nonsmokers. The target customer for

ESDs is the adult smoker who wants to quit, cut down, or be able to vape in areas where smoking is prohibited. "We don't need to create new customers," explains Mike Floorwalker, who runs a vape shop in Louisville, Colorado. "Ninety-five percent of our customers are ex-smokers, meaning the tobacco industry has created plenty of customers for us and will continue to do so for a long time."[34]

Research has confirmed this—most surveys show that at least 90 percent of vapers are also smokers or ex-smokers. For instance, a 2013 study published in the *Journal of Environmental Research and Public Health* found that, out of the more than forty-five hundred vapers surveyed, 91.1 percent were former smokers. Geoff Braithwaite, owner of the e-liquid manufacturer Tasty Vapor, explains it this way: "Our target customer base is those people who felt doomed to a life of smoking."[35]

> ## "We don't need to create new customers."[34]
>
> —Mike Floorwalker, who runs a vape shop in Colorado.

An examination of ESD ads supports the industry's claim. As the Consumer Advocates for Smoke-Free Alternatives Association (CASAA) explains, "Often overlooked by critics in these ads are the claims about the ability to 'smoke anywhere' and have a safer/healthier option to smoking—a clear indication that they are targeting current smokers and smokers concerned about their health and not new/young smokers."[36] One example of this is a 2014 ad for blu e-cigarettes. Spokesperson Jenny McCarthy describes how e-cigarettes have improved her life as a smoker. "Now when I go to public places that don't allow smoking, I can whip out my blu and know that I won't scare any guys away."[37] The ad talks about how blu e-cigarettes can improve the social and sex life of current smokers, who will no longer be ostracized for their habit. Even though McCarthy is a celebrity, the ad is clearly targeting current smokers, not young people who do not smoke.

One reason critics may believe that ESD advertising targets minors is that ESD commercials attempt to make the devices seem cool. However, advertisers use this technique to sell many adult products, including cars, cell phones, and alcohol. In addition, the smokers' demographic (characteristics of the group) is very similar to the typical demographic for a teenager. Dr. Michael Rabinoff notes that studies have shown that smokers are more likely to be "risk-taking, extroverted, defiant, and impulsive"[38]—characteristics that can also be applied to the average teenager. This may make it seem as though an ad is targeting young people when it is actually reaching out to adult smokers.

The ESD Industry Self-Regulates

The ESD industry has committed to not selling to children and as a result has taken several steps toward self-regulation. "We card anybody who doesn't look over 25 years old," says Floorwalker. "I know of no other shop—in my state or any other—that doesn't do the same."[39] Even in states where it is legal for minors to purchase ESDs, many vape shops still will not sell to anyone under eighteen and have policies in place to card young people even though it is not legally required. As one employee at a Michigan vape shop explained to an underage customer, "We have to make sure you're over 18. We're just getting into the habit of doing it for when they actually make it law."[40]

The industry also protects children from its products by packaging e-liquids in shrink-wrap and using childproof caps to prevent younger children from accidentally drinking the liquid nicotine. In fact, because of the increased demand from the e-liquid industry, childproof cap manufacturers are having trouble keeping supplies in stock. E-liquids are also labeled with warnings such as "May contain nicotine. Keep away from children and pets. For use by adults 18+," though this also is not yet required by the FDA. As Floorwalker explains, "We know that we are selling an adult product, and we want to stay in business."[41]

Adults Enjoy Sweet Flavors, Too

The ESD industry also denies the accusation that it is luring children into trying its product by using sweet flavors. In fact, it created sweet flavors at the request of adult smokers—not as a way to addict minors to vaping. "It's nearly impossible to replicate the taste of a real cigarette in a liquid form,"[42] explains John Madden, a vaper who writes for Ecigarette-Reviewed. He says that the flavor from a tobacco cigarette is affected

Most Adult Vapers Prefer Sweet Flavors

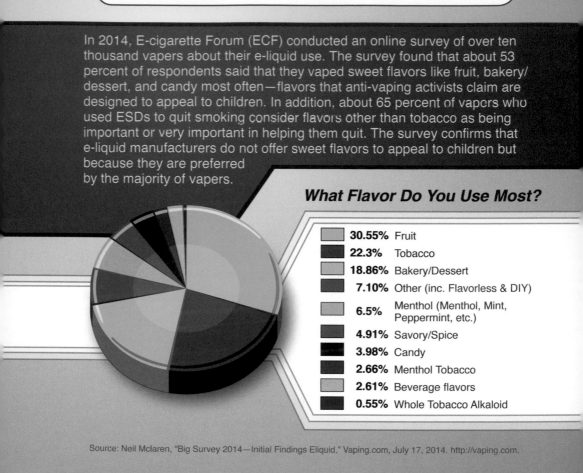

In 2014, E-cigarette Forum (ECF) conducted an online survey of over ten thousand vapers about their e-liquid use. The survey found that about 53 percent of respondents said that they vaped sweet flavors like fruit, bakery/dessert, and candy most often—flavors that anti-vaping activists claim are designed to appeal to children. In addition, about 65 percent of vapers who used ESDs to quit smoking consider flavors other than tobacco as being important or very important in helping them quit. The survey confirms that e-liquid manufacturers do not offer sweet flavors to appeal to children but because they are preferred by the majority of vapers.

What Flavor Do You Use Most?

- **30.55%** Fruit
- **22.3%** Tobacco
- **18.86%** Bakery/Dessert
- **7.10%** Other (inc. Flavorless & DIY)
- **6.5%** Menthol (Menthol, Mint, Peppermint, etc.)
- **4.91%** Savory/Spice
- **3.98%** Candy
- **2.66%** Menthol Tobacco
- **2.61%** Beverage flavors
- **0.55%** Whole Tobacco Alkaloid

Source: Neil Mclaren, "Big Survey 2014—Initial Findings Eliquid," Vaping.com, July 17, 2014. http://vaping.com.

by the thousands of chemicals and additives present in the smoke—and since the tobacco is combusting, there is a burning flavor as well that cannot be easily replicated. According to CASAA, "Adults, who make up the majority of electronic cigarette consumers, specifically requested alternative flavors that would work well with the liquid base."[43] Since that base was propylene glycol and glycerin—which naturally has a slightly sweet taste—fruit, dessert, and candy flavors tasted the best.

It turns out that ex-smokers actually prefer these sweet and fruity flavors. A 2013 survey by E-cigarette Forum found that three-quarters of respondents preferred flavors other than tobacco. These flavors included fruit (31 percent) and bakery/dessert (19 percent). And sales data from fourteen Palm Beach Vapors stores revealed that only two of the stores' top nineteen sellers were tobacco flavors, which came in eighteenth and nineteenth on the list.

Adult vapers say that these flavors are key to making vaping a pleasurable experience—and a viable replacement for tobacco cigarettes. A poll by CASAA found that about half of adult vapers polled said that nontobacco flavors are the reason they do not return to tobacco. After vaping the sweeter flavors, respondents said, tobacco cigarettes no longer tasted good or had as much appeal. And a 2013 study published in the *Journal of Environmental Research and Public Health* found that "the majority reported that restricting variability [in flavors] will make ECs [electronic cigarettes] less enjoyable and more boring, while 48.5 percent mentioned that it would increase craving for cigarettes and 39.7 percent said that it would have been less likely for them to reduce or quit smoking."[44] Clearly, having access to a variety of flavors—including sweet flavors—is an important part of making a successful switch from tobacco cigarettes to ESDs.

Catering to Adult Needs

Finally, not all e-liquids come in flavors named after candy. Some are complex blends of both sweet and savory flavors, some are spicy, and some taste like alcoholic drinks or adult-oriented gourmet desserts. This variety of flavors is one reason ESDs have become so popular among adults. As Madden writes, "Just because we age does not mean we lose interest in the delectables of life. Flavored e-cigs undoubtedly taste better than tar-filled tobacco smoke and are a sincere attempt to keep health conscious smokers from falling off the vapor wagon."[45]

The ESD industry does not target children—not in its advertising and not by adding sweet flavorings to e-liquid.

> "Just because we age does not mean we lose interest in the delectables of life."[45]
>
> —John Madden, a vaper, on why sweet e-liquid flavors appeal to adults.

ESDs are adult products designed for adult smokers who want to quit or cut down on their smoking. However, ESDs are also electronic devices—and some people believe this is the real reason for their popularity among young people. "There's going to be that novelty around it—it's a brand new thing, it's an electronic device," says Braithwaite. "That kind of stuff will always appeal to kids; it would have appealed to me."[46]

Chapter Three

Are E-cigarettes and Vaping a Gateway to Tobacco Products?

E-cigarettes and Vaping Are a Gateway to Tobacco Products

- ESDs and vaping sustain nicotine addiction in smokers and cause addiction in nonsmokers, which can lead to later tobacco use.
- ESDs make "smoking" acceptable and destigmatize smoking in public places.
- ESDs increase interest in smoking tobacco cigarettes among nonsmokers.

The Debate at a Glance

E-cigarettes and Vaping Are Not a Gateway to Tobacco Products

- Studies that take vaping frequency into account show that ESDs do not lead to tobacco use among nonsmokers.
- Many studies that claim that ESDs are a gateway to smoking misread the data.
- The nicotine added to e-liquids is not strongly addictive.

E-cigarettes and Vaping Are a Gateway to Tobacco Products

"[Vaping] actually increases interest in smoking, and that's kind of the smoking gun, no pun intended."

—Thomas Wills is codirector of the Cancer Prevention and Control Program at the University of Hawaii Cancer Center.

Quoted in Cameron Scott, "Worst Fears About Teen E-cigarette Use Justified, New Data Suggest," Healthline News, December 15, 2014. www.healthline.com.

Consider these questions as you read:

1. How persuasive is the argument that teen vaping can lead to tobacco use? Explain your answer.
2. Do you agree that the popularity of vaping is making smoking cigarettes seem more acceptable? Explain your answer.
3. Is it reasonable to conclude that vaping is a gateway to smoking because kids who vape are more likely to say that they will try cigarettes in the future? Explain your answer.

Editor's note: The discussion that follows presents common arguments made in support of this perspective, reinforced by facts, quotes, and examples taken from various sources.

Teenagers have been taking up vaping at an alarming rate. In California a survey of 450,000 students undertaken during the 2013–2014 school year found that 29 percent had tried ESDs. Hawaii also reports that 29 percent of its students have tried ESDs. In fact, ESDs have surpassed tobacco cigarettes as the most commonly used nicotine product among young people, with 450,000 middle school students and 2 million high school students now vaping. Experts are concerned that this explosion of ESD use among children and teens is creating a gateway to tobacco use—both by renormalizing and destigmatizing smoking and by addicting a new generation to nicotine. Once addicted, these young people will be more likely to switch to cigarettes and other dangerous tobacco products in the future.

ESDs Sustain Nicotine Addiction

One concern about the rise in ESD use among children and teens is that it discourages those who do smoke from quitting nicotine. Tobacco use among young people has dropped steadily over the past few years: A CDC survey found that 9.2 percent of students used tobacco cigarettes in 2014, down from 15.8 percent in 2011. However, e-cigarette use rose to 13.4 percent in 2014, up from only 1.5 percent in 2011. This means that many students who would otherwise quit nicotine products have instead switched to vaping.

Nicotine is especially dangerous for young people because their brains are still developing. This can make them especially sensitive to nicotine's addictive effects. According to Ron Chapman, director of the California Department of Public Health, "Research shows that adolescent smokers report some symptoms of dependence even at low levels of cigarette consumption."[47] This means that young people can become addicted to nicotine faster, and experience a stronger level of addiction, than they would if they started using nicotine as adults.

> "Exposure to nicotine enhances the rewarding effects of other drugs."[48]
>
> —Nora Volkow, head of the National Institute on Drug Abuse.

Nicotine use has also been found to lead to other addictions—in part because it can make drugs like alcohol, marijuana, and narcotics more enjoyable. Nora Volkow, who heads the National Institute on Drug Abuse, explains, "Research has shown that exposure to nicotine enhances the rewarding effects of other drugs. . . . [Public health experts are] concerned that in turn, it [nicotine] may serve as a so-called gateway drug."[48]

Not all e-liquid contains nicotine, and some people claim that teens are more likely to vape zero-nicotine e-liquid because nicotine interferes with the taste. However, anecdotal evidence suggests that even young teenagers are now deliberately using nicotine as a way to relax or deal with daily stresses. As fourteen-year-old Rebecca says, "I like vaping because it helps me with stress, with drama at school, with drama at home, with getting overwhelmed at school as in all the work and practice with basketball and sports."[49] Vaping has become so acceptable that teens can dose themselves with nicotine during the school day without being criticized by their peers. In fact, some middle schoolers report that the reason people start vaping is to be cool or to fit in. This means that teens who smoke are no longer under pressure by their peers to break their addiction to nicotine (by quitting tobacco products). Instead, they switch to vaping and sustain their addiction.

> "I like vaping because it helps me with stress."[49]
>
> —Rebecca, a fourteen-year-old who vapes in school.

ESDs Make Public "Smoking" Normal Again

Another criticism of ESDs is that their visibility in society threatens to renormalize smoking. Cigarette smoking was once so common in society that it was even allowed in hospitals and on airplanes. Now, after several decades of antismoking campaigns, public cigarette smoking is restricted to outdoor smoking areas. As researchers write in the *New England Journal of Medicine*, "The once-widespread habit didn't simply become denormalized or marginalized; it became highly stigmatized."[50] However, ESDs are making the act of smoking acceptable again. In other words, the phenomenon of vaping at work, in restaurants, in school, or in other places where smoking is prohibited is in itself creating a gateway to the renormalization of tobacco smoking.

Claire Micks, an ex-smoker who does not use ESDs, believes this has already happened. Micks found her three-year-old daughter pretending to vape with a pipe cleaner because she had witnessed so much ESD use in public. "I don't want my daughter to grow up thinking that smoking of any kind is cool. Is adult. Is what people 'do,'" she writes. "If my daughter grows up thinking that those little white sticks [e-cigarettes] are the norm, what's to stop her wanting to try out the real thing?"[51]

Rising E-cigarette Use Will Eventually Lead to More Teen Smoking

At present, e-cigarettes are far more popular among youth than traditional tobacco cigarettes. While this sounds like good news, it is not. The nicotine in e-cigarettes is addictive and, according to the FDA, will likely lead teens to start or resume smoking tobacco cigarettes in the future. This concern grows out of the National Youth Tobacco Survey, which found that use of e-cigarettes tripled among middle and high school students between 2013 and 2014. The survey shows that students who otherwise would have quit tobacco and nicotine products altogether instead switched to e-cigarettes. Many of these teens are likely to return to traditional tobacco cigarettes to satisfy their nicotine cravings.

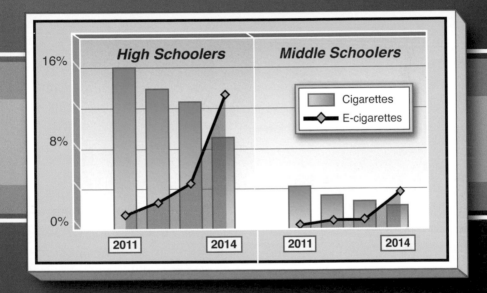

Source: Brady Dennis, "E-cigarette Use Triples Among Middle and High School Students, Study Says," *Washington Post*, April 16, 2015. www.washingtonpost.com.

ESDs Increase Interest in Smoking

Another concern about ESDs is that children who have never smoked are using them and will go on to try tobacco products. Research is beginning to support this theory. A 2015 University of Michigan study of forty thousand teens found that 8.7 percent of fourteen-year-olds had tried an e-cigarette, whereas only 4 percent had tried tobacco cigarettes. This implies that most teens who use e-cigarettes have never smoked cigarettes before. Although these kids may be simply experimenting, even intermittent exposure to nicotine puts them at risk of addiction. As CDC director Dr. Tom Frieden warns, "Many teens who start with e-cigarettes may be condemned to struggling with a lifelong addiction to nicotine and conventional cigarettes."[52]

Kids who vape are also more likely to say that they would try tobacco cigarettes in the future. According to a 2014 report by the CDC, 44 percent of nonsmoking kids who vape said they intend to smoke tobacco cigarettes, compared to 22 percent who had never tried ESDs. And a 2014 study published in Wales found that ten-year-olds who had tried ESDs were seven times more likely to say that they might start smoking cigarettes in the next two years than those who had never tried ESDs. Profiles of these young people suggest that, in the absence of ESDs, they probably would not use tobacco products. According to Thomas Wills, codirector of the Cancer Prevention and Control Program at the University of Hawaii Cancer Center, "Our interpretation is that e-cigs may be operating to recruit relatively low-risk people to smoking."[53]

A Pathway to Smoking

ESD use among nonsmokers increases their interest in smoking and exposes them to the highly addictive drug nicotine. For these reasons, ESDs are a gateway to tobacco use among teens who do not smoke. "E-cigs seem to be a stimulus, which is what the prevention community was predicting a year ago, which is that this is just a pathway [to cigarette smoking],"[54] says educational researcher Barbara Dietsch. For teens who do smoke, ESDs allow them to continue their nicotine addiction instead of quitting. They are more likely to be "dual users" (people who both smoke cigarettes and vape) and still suffer the devastating health consequences of using tobacco products. ESDs also act as a gateway to renormalization of smoking in public spaces in society, removing the stigma around smoking that has encouraged so many people to quit. For these reasons, ESDs should be considered a gateway drug to more dangerous tobacco products.

E-cigarettes and Vaping Are Not a Gateway to Tobacco Products

"Young people are certainly experimenting with e-cigarettes. . . . However, our data show that at the moment this experimentation is not translating into regular use."

—Linda Bauld is a professor and the deputy director of UK Centre for Tobacco and Alcohol Studies.

Quoted in Cancer Research UK, "Research Shows Most Children Do Not Regularly Use E-cigarettes," June 12, 2015. www.cancerresearchuk.org.

Consider these questions as you read:

1. How convincing is the argument that e-cigarettes and vaping are not a gateway to smoking? Explain your answer.
2. Can study results be skewed by how questions are worded? Explain your answer and come up with an example of differently worded questions that seek the same information but could lead to different results.
3. What do you think about one expert's idea to raise levels of nicotine in ESDs to make them more appealing as a stop-smoking aid? Explain.

Editor's note: The discussion that follows presents common arguments made in support of this perspective, reinforced by facts, quotes, and examples taken from various sources.

One reason so many antitobacco activists oppose ESDs is because they believe young people who vape will eventually switch to tobacco cigarettes. This idea is based on the belief that nicotine is extremely addictive; experts have equated the difficulty of quitting nicotine with quitting heroin or other highly addictive narcotics. However, when frequency of ESD use is taken into account, studies reveal that nonsmoking adolescents only experiment with ESDs. They do not go on to vape—or smoke—regularly.

Studies Show ESD Use Does Not Lead to Smoking

Despite headlines to the contrary, studies that support the idea that ESDs are not a gateway to smoking are much better designed than those that indicate they are. For instance, in Great Britain a 2015 YouGov survey of 2,178 young people aged eleven to eighteen found that regular vaping among nonsmokers was virtually nonexistent. Of the young people who had never smoked a cigarette, 99 percent reported never having tried ESDs and 1 percent reported trying them once or twice. The small number who regularly use ESDs, according to the study, are either current or previous smokers. In addition, only 1 percent of nonsmoking children say that they might try an electronic cigarette soon. Deborah Arnott, chief executive of Action on Smoking and Health, a UK health charity, says of the study results, "While it is clearly important to continue to monitor both smoking rates and use of electronic cigarettes in adults and children, so far there is no evidence that use of electronic cigarettes is proving to be a gateway into smoking."[55]

In fact, the primary motivation for using ESDs appears to be to quit smoking. This is supported by a Harvard School of Public Health study of 26,500 consumers across Europe. The Harvard study found that 20 percent of smokers and 4 percent of former smokers had tried an ESD at least once, but only 1.1 percent of nonsmokers had tried ESDs. The study, the largest of its kind, concluded that although ESD users were primarily young—between fifteen and twenty-four years old—they were almost exclusively heavy smokers who were using the devices to quit smoking. In fact, the study found that smokers who had attempted to quit in the previous year were two times as likely to have tried ESDs as smokers who were not trying to quit.

Many Studies Misread the Data

Studies that have attempted to find a connection between ESD use and traditional cigarettes are hampered by either flawed methodology or by inaccurate reading of the results. For instance, in 2014 Stanton Glantz, director of the Center for Tobacco Control Research and Education at the University of California–San Francisco, surveyed US adolescents and

Nicotine in E-cigarettes Less Addictive than in Tobacco Cigarettes

A 2014 study published in *Scientific Reports* found that nicotine is absorbed by the body much more slowly from ESDs than it is from tobacco cigarettes. Researchers found that smoking a cigarette for five minutes resulted in blood plasma nicotine levels 286 and 185 percent higher than when using first-generation and new-generation ESDs, respectively (new-generation devices deliver more vapor, and therefore more nicotine). It took thirty-five minutes of vaping a new-generation ESD to reach comparable levels. This indicates that ESDs are less addictive than tobacco cigarettes and deliver nicotine at a similar rate to nicotine replacement therapies like nicotine gum, which makes it unlikely that ESDs would lead to tobacco use.

Comparison of nicotine absorption rates after ESD vs. tobacco use

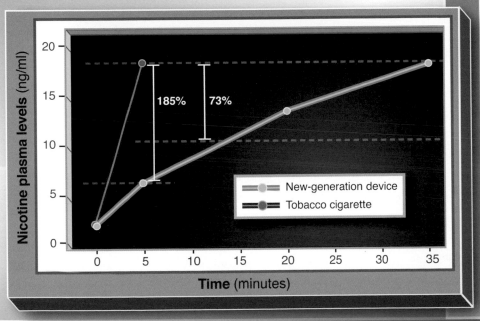

Source: Konstantinos Farsalinos et al., "Nicotine Absorption from Electronic Cigarette Use: Comparison Between First- and New-Generation Devices," *Nature*, February 26, 2014.

found that those who used ESDs were more likely to be heavy smokers. From these data, Glantz concluded, "E-cigarette use is aggravating rather than ameliorating the tobacco epidemic among youths."[56] However, Glantz had uncovered only a correlation between vaping and heavy smoking; he did not find that using ESDs in any way caused heavy smoking or prevented people from quitting. In fact, the study may have simply revealed that people who smoke heavily are more likely to use ESDs.

When trying to identify ESD usage patterns, researchers also often fail to ask people how frequently they vape. According to Dr. Michael Siegel, a former employee of the CDC's Office on Smoking and Health, the CDC asks about use in the past thirty days. Siegel explains that this indicates only that people—especially teens—are experimenting with ESDs. When a study does identify regular vapers—as the YouGov survey in Great Britain does—it usually finds no evidence that vaping leads to smoking. Many ESD advocates agree with Siegel, including the authors of a 2015 article published in *Tobacco Control*. Researchers looked at the problem of identifying vaping frequency and concluded, "Defining . . . prevalence as any use in the past 30 days may include experimenters unlikely to continue use." They said that using this criterion had "questionable utility"[57] for tracking public health trends.

> "It didn't seem as though [e-cigarette use] really proved to be a gateway to anything." [58]
>
> — Ted Wagener, a psychologist at the University of Oklahoma Health Sciences Center.

Very few studies actually deal directly with the question of whether vaping leads to smoking—for instance, by asking adolescent smokers whether they started with ESDs. In one such study in 2013, led by Ted Wagener, a psychologist at the University of Oklahoma Health Sciences Center, twelve hundred college students were asked specifically about whether ESD use led to tobacco use. Only one student who had used an ESD as a nonsmoker went on to smoke cigarettes regularly. Most of the remaining forty-two nonsmokers who said they had tried e-cigarettes no longer used any nicotine or tobacco products. "It didn't seem as though [e-cigarette use] really proved to be a gateway to anything,"[58] says Wagener.

Nicotine in ESDs Is Much Less Addictive than in Tobacco

The idea that people who use ESDs will go on to use tobacco products stems from the perceived power of nicotine addiction. Experts have equated the difficulty in quitting nicotine with quitting heroin or other highly addictive narcotics. However, the liquid nicotine found in e-liquids is less addictive than nicotine found in tobacco leaves. This is because liquid nicotine has been isolated from the substances present in the tobacco plant that produces it. According to Dr. Paul Newhouse, director of Vanderbilt University's Center for Cognitive Medicine, nicotine gets a boost from these substances—and tobacco companies add additional chemicals to further boost the drug's effect. "People won't smoke without nicotine in cigarettes, but they won't take nicotine by itself," says Newhouse. "Nicotine is not reinforcing enough. That's why FDA agreed nicotine could be sold over the counter [in the form of smoking-cessation aids]. No one wants to take it because it's not pleasant enough by itself. And it's hard to get animals [in a lab] to self-administer nicotine the way they will with cocaine."[59]

Nicotine is also a fairly benign substance when isolated from tobacco. Newhouse notes that it has virtually no side effects. When administered to Alzheimer's patients and people suffering from mental decline, it improved their cognitive function without causing addiction. "It seems very safe even in nonsmokers," Newhouse says. "In our studies we find it actually reduces blood pressure chronically. And there were no addiction or withdrawal problems, and nobody started smoking cigarettes. The risk of addiction to nicotine alone is virtually nil."[60]

> "The risk of addiction to nicotine alone is virtually nil."[60]
>
> —Dr. Paul Newhouse, director of Vanderbilt University's Center for Cognitive Medicine.

Studies have also shown that nicotine is absorbed more slowly when vaped than when smoked. A 2014 study published in *Scientific Reports* notes that it takes thirty-five minutes of vaping to raise the level of nicotine in the blood to the degree achieved by five minutes of smoking a tobacco cigarette. This implies that vaping is not as psychologically rewarding as smoking and is therefore less addictive. Public health officials have even discussed the idea of raising the nicotine levels of ESDs (through regulation) to make them more rewarding—which would make them more effective as a smoking-cessation tool. Vaughan Rees, interim director of the Harvard T.H. Chan School of Public Health's

Center for Global Tobacco Control, supports this idea. He believes that higher levels of nicotine would give smokers enough of a reward to be able to quit smoking, while the nicotine itself would interfere with the mild, pleasant flavor of e-liquids, discouraging ESD use among young people. He says, "We're eager to find the sweet spot [in nicotine levels] where we support switching away from tobacco cigarettes without unintentionally increasing an individual's nicotine dependence."[61]

No Evidence that Vaping Leads to Smoking

The assertion that ESDs are a gateway to cigarette smoking is not supported by current science. There is no credible evidence that nonsmokers will start smoking after trying ESDs, nor is there any evidence that nonsmokers are becoming regular vapers. This is likely because ESDs provide a lower level of nicotine reward compared to tobacco cigarettes, which makes them comparable to smoking-cessation tools like nicotine patches and gum that are currently on the market.

Chapter Four

How Should E-cigarettes and Vaping Be Regulated?

E-cigarettes and Vaping Need Tighter Regulation

- Regulation would protect minors by limiting exposure to advertising and access to products.
- A requirement to use childproof packaging would prevent small children from being poisoned by liquid nicotine.
- Manufacturers must be required to make sure that nicotine concentrations match labels on e-liquids.

The Debate at a Glance

Tighter Regulation of E-cigarettes and Vaping Is Not Needed

- Strict regulation has unintended consequences, like encouraging people to continue to smoke cigarettes.
- Strict regulation will be so costly that only big companies will survive.
- Many entities that support the FDA's rules stand to profit from strict regulation.

E-cigarettes and Vaping Need Tighter Regulation

"Most consumers would be shocked to realize the products [ESDs and e-liquids] they buy have less oversight than a bag of dog food, and are often manufactured and imported from countries that have histories of tainted pharmaceutical and food products."

—Nathan Cobb is a pulmonologist at Georgetown University School of Medicine.

Quoted in Maggie Fox, "What's So Bad About E-cigarettes?," NBC News, April 25, 2014. www.nbcnews.com.

Consider these questions as you read:

1. How persuasive is the argument that e-cigarettes and vaping need tighter regulation? Explain your answer.
2. Why does information presented on product labels matter? Provide examples to support your answer.
3. Do you think advertising or prominent placement in convenience stores make teens want to try ESDs? Explain your answer.

Editor's note: The discussion that follows presents common arguments made in support of this perspective, reinforced by facts, quotes, and examples taken from various sources.

Weak e-cigarette regulations have been a boon to manufacturers and sellers but represent a threat to consumers. Most states have already banned direct sales of e-cigarettes to minors, but this has not stopped young people from buying ESDs online. Manufacturers have also benefited by not having to test ESDs and e-liquids for harmful substances, list ingredients, adhere to good manufacturing practices, or protect children from ingesting the toxic nicotine in their products. For these reasons—and because ESDs contain nicotine—they should be regulated like tobacco products.

Young People Can Easily Buy E-cigarettes Online

Even though most states have banned sales to minors, young people are still able to buy ESDs and e-liquids online. Some in the ESD industry claim that, because teens must be at least eighteen to legally have a credit card in their own name, it is already difficult enough for young people to buy these products on the Internet. But because online purchasing is so popular, most parents give their teens access to a credit card long before they are eighteen. A 2013 survey by the investment bank Piper Jaffray found that 79 percent of teen females and 76 percent of teen males said they shop online. This means that young people can easily purchase ESD products from the hundreds of online storefronts that sell them—and it is perfectly legal for them to do so.

Some states have tried to solve this problem by requiring online retailers operating in their state to use age-verification software. However, so far this requirement has not been an effective deterrent. In a 2015 study published in *JAMA Pediatrics*, teenagers were recruited to try to purchase ESDs from ninety-eight online vendors. In 94 percent of cases, the teens were able to do so using an adult's credit card. And of the ninety-eight vendors, only seven used age-verification software. Even more concerning is the fact that this software was effective only in a single instance. Teens in the study were still able to place orders on six out of the seven websites that used age-verification software.

Restricting Access Will Change Public Perception

Even if online sales were banned or severely restricted, the way that brick-and-mortar stores currently promote e-cigarettes gives young people the impression that they are harmless. Many stores display e-cigarettes prominently on their checkout counters, and some even place them near candy and other products that appeal to children. Because of this, young people are much more likely to perceive ESDs as a safe alternative to

ESD Regulation Has Strong Support

CS Mott Children's Hospital's National Poll on Children's Health surveyed about twenty-one hundred adults and found strong support for regulation of the ESD industry. About nine out of ten adults supported requirements for safety testing and prohibiting sales to minors, and about eight out of ten supported regulating ESDs like other nicotine products.

Public Support for Electronic Cigarette Laws, 2013

Require manufacturers to test for safety	88%
Prohibit the sale to people younger than 18	86%
FDA regulation like other nicotine products	77%
Restrict marketing on social networking sites	71%
Prohibit use in indoor places and workplaces	64%

Source: "E-cigarettes Laws Just Smokescreen? Teens Easily Work Around Bans by Buying E-cigarettes Online," National Poll on Children's Health, March 4, 2015.

smoking—or even as a sweet treat instead of a dangerous product that contains nicotine.

Displaying e-cigarettes on checkout counters not only encourages use by minors, it gives adults the impression that e-cigarettes are as harmless as candy. Because of this, adults are less likely to discourage e-cigarette use among young people. Some parents even buy their kids e-cigarettes to discourage them from smoking. According to vape shop owner Mike Floorwalker, "I personally have dealt with dozens of parents who wanted to buy a device for their teenager."[62] These parents may not be aware of the risks that these products pose to their children—in part because they are not physically sold alongside other tobacco products.

Liquid Nicotine Endangers Children

Many e-liquids come in flavors that appeal to children (such as fruit, dessert, and candy), and most have a sweet smell. Because of this, children can accidentally drink them—which can be fatal. According to Lee Cantrell, director of the San Diego division of the California Poison Control System, "[Nicotine] is one of the most potent naturally occurring toxins we have."[63] In liquid form, nicotine can be swallowed or absorbed through the skin in much greater concentrations than when inhaled. Symptoms of nicotine poisoning are agitation, drooling, vomiting, difficulty breathing, convulsions, coma, and in some cases, death. According to the medical journal *Tobacco Control*, the fatal dose of nicotine for adults is 30 to 60 milligrams and for children is 10 milligrams—an amount found in a typical bottle of e-liquid.

The ESD industry claims that nearly all manufacturers use child-proof containers to keep children safe from exposure to liquid nicotine products. However, this has not been enough to protect children from accidental poisoning. As e-cigarettes have gained popularity, calls to poison control centers about nicotine poisoning have skyrocketed, from 271 calls in 2011 to 3,957 calls in 2014. About half of those calls were about nicotine exposure in children. Hospitalizations due to accidental exposure are also on the rise; three times as many people were hospitalized due to nicotine poisoning in 2013 as in 2012. And tragically, at least one child has died as a direct result of drinking e-liquid. On December 9, 2014, in Fort Plain, New York, an eighteen-month-old boy went into convulsions shortly after drinking a bottle of e-liquid and died in the hospital.

> "[Nicotine] is one of the most potent naturally occurring toxins we have."[63]
>
> —Lee Cantrell, director of the San Diego division of the California Poison Control System.

At the root of the problem of accidental overdose is the fact that many parents do not realize that liquid nicotine is highly poisonous. In the Fort Plain poisoning, the bottle of e-liquid—which did not have a childproof cap—was accidentally left open within the child's reach. An adult who would never dream of leaving an open bottle of prescription drugs in reach of a toddler might not realize that less than a teaspoon of e-liquid can poison a child. This is especially true if there is no warning label on the bottle, which is frequently the case. According to Ashley Webb, director of the Kentucky Regional Poison Control Center at Kosair Children's Hospital, which has treated many children for nicotine poisoning, "A lot of parents didn't realize it [e-liquid] was toxic until the kid started vomiting."[64]

E-liquid Labeling Is Not Accurate

Another problem with the lack of regulation of e-liquids is that manufacturers have not been required to make sure that labeled nicotine concentrations are accurate. This means that consumers often do not know how much nicotine they are inhaling, which can exacerbate addiction and make ESDs useless as a stop-smoking aid. Studies have found that mislabeling of nicotine content is a frequent occurrence. For instance, a 2015 study by the Salt Lake County Health Department in Utah found that 61 percent of e-liquid purchased locally was mislabeled by at least 10 percent. In fact, one of the samples labeled as "nicotine free" actually contained 7.35 milligrams per milliliter.

> "A lot of parents didn't realize it [e-liquid] was toxic until the kid started vomiting."[64]
>
> —Ashley Webb, director of the Kentucky Regional Poison Control Center at Kosair Children's Hospital.

According to Tyler McCanus, an ESD advocate who writes for the website Electronic Cigarette Consumer Reviews, "The problem is the boutique brands or e-juices that are blended by well intentioned but unqualified people who are mixing and bottling the ingredients in a non-laboratory setting."[65] In fact, some vape shops have their salespeople add liquid nicotine to e-liquids at the time of purchase, mixing custom blends in the back of the store. Inaccurate labeling not only puts vapers at risk of worsening their nicotine addiction, it can prevent poison control and hospital staff from effectively treating nicotine overdoses in children, which can have deadly results.

The Public Must Be Protected

If ESD products were classified as tobacco products and regulated in the same way as cigarettes, many commonsense safety measures would automatically be put in place. For instance, sales to minors would be banned nationwide, and online retailers would be forced to verify a consumer's age both online and upon delivery. To limit exposure to young people, e-cigarettes would be sold alongside cigarettes and not displayed on sales counters with products that appeal to children. Childproof caps, warning labels, and accurate labeling of nicotine levels would be required. In addition, producers would have to prove that they followed safe manufacturing practices and would have to disclose all ingredients and prove their safety. Whether the FDA will take this necessary step remains to be seen.

Tighter Regulation of E-cigarettes and Vaping Is Not Needed

"Excessive regulation of e-cigarettes would protect the market monopoly of cigarettes and have the potential consequences of disease in and death of millions of smokers."

—Peter Hajek is a scientist at the Tobacco Dependence Research Unit at St. Bartholomew's Hospital and the London School of Medicine and Dentistry.

Quoted in Sarah Cassidy, "'Alarmist' E-cigarette Report Attacked by Tobacco Health Expert," *Independent* (London), August 18, 2015. www.independent.co.uk.

Consider these questions as you read:

1. How convincing is the argument that ESDs do not need tighter regulation? Explain your answer.
2. Is the argument that premarket review should not be required because it would destroy most of the ESD industry supported by the essay? Why or why not?
3. In your opinion, which is more important: protecting children from ESDs or encouraging smokers to use the devices to quit smoking? Explain.

Editor's note: The discussion that follows presents common arguments made in support of this perspective, reinforced by facts, quotes, and examples taken from various sources.

The ESD industry supports regulation that protects minors. "Childproof packaging and warning labels—those we've always considered the cost of doing business. That makes sense, and they should be implemented,"[66] says Tony Reed, owner of Indigo Vapor of South Bend, Indiana. However, categorizing ESDs as tobacco products and subjecting them to the same laws as cigarettes is unnecessary and excessive. It sends the message that

ESDs are as dangerous as cigarettes and discourages people from quitting smoking. It also will put all but the largest ESD manufacturers—tobacco companies—out of business, which will eliminate the innovation that has made the products such a popular alternative to smoking.

Fewer Smokers Will Quit

Regulating ESDs like tobacco products can have the unintended consequence of discouraging people from using ESDs as a way to quit smoking. Nearly all vapers are smokers or ex-smokers, and most use ESDs to cut down on or eliminate their smoking habit. For many, ESDs have been the only product that has been successful in enabling them to quit smoking. For instance, sixty-four-year-old Mike Cline, a longtime smoker, tried vaping when his son suggested it as an alternative to smoking. "I haven't wanted a cigarette since then," he said. "This has been a miracle."[67]

One reason that ex-smokers like Cline have success with ESDs is because they can control the amount of nicotine they inhale—making ESDs much more satisfying than nicotine patches or gum. Regulations that would limit nicotine concentrations in e-liquids because of fears of accidental poisoning would mean fewer people would find ESDs a satisfying alternative to cigarettes. Overstated health-warning statements, limits on advertising, using taxes as a disincentive, and outlawing Internet sales would also discourage quitting—by making ESDs, or information about ESDs, harder to come by.

> "I haven't wanted a cigarette since [switching to vaping]."[67]
>
> —Longtime smoker Mike Cline.

Strict regulations would also influence public perception about how harmful ESDs actually are. This effect is already apparent—public perception that ESDs are dangerous is on the rise. A 2014 study published in the *American Journal of Preventive Medicine* found that in 2010, 84.7 percent of current smokers believed that cigarettes were more harmful than ESDs. Due to media coverage of the efforts of anti-vaping advocates to regulate ESDs, that number dropped to 65 percent in 2013. This means that 45 percent of smokers see no health benefit in switching

New Rules Attempt to Solve Nonexistent Problem

Secondhand smoke from cigarettes is a scientifically documented health hazard. As can be seen in this chart, secondhand vapor from ESDs does not represent a threat. In fact, levels of the carcinogen formaldehyde in secondhand vapor are less than amounts found in average indoor/outdoor air. Yet some government agencies have proposed regulations that treat ESDs just like cigarettes—for example, prohibiting vaping in public places. This is a clear-cut example of rules being made to solve a problem that does not exist. Such rules are unnecessary.

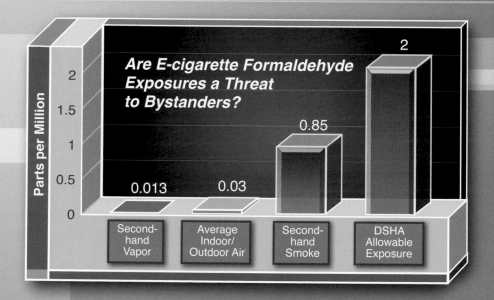

Are E-cigarette Formaldehyde Exposures a Threat to Bystanders?

Secondhand Vapor	Average Indoor/Outdoor Air	Secondhand Smoke	DSHA Allowable Exposure
0.013	0.03	0.85	2

Parts per Million

to ESDs—even though there have been no definitive studies about the health hazards of ESDs, and even though switching could potentially save their lives. Jon Deak, CEO of Electronic Cigarette Consumer Reviews and a staunch vaping advocate, says that anti-vaping laws put people's lives at risk. He says of a proposed bill in California to regulate ESDs, "If one smoker out there today hears that California Public Health has declared e-cigs to be a health threat and decides to keep smoking cigarettes because he or she comes under the impression that e-cigs are just as bad as tobacco, that person has just been condemned to a life of potentially increased health risks."[68]

Regulating ESDs like cigarettes also means that secondhand vapor, which is relatively harmless, would be treated like secondhand smoke, which is a health hazard. According to Bill Godshall, executive director of Smokefree Pennsylvania, laws that ban indoor vaping would "prompt many vapers to go outside to smoking areas and be exposed to second-hand smoke [from cigarette smokers] once again."[69] It would also eliminate a major benefit of ESDs—being able to use nicotine without having to go outdoors.

Strict Regulation Will Destroy the Industry

The requirement that ESDs be tested as stringently as cigarettes, known as premarket review, would put the manufacturers who make the most popular ESDs—personal vaporizers that can be filled with more than seven thousand flavors of e-liquids—out of business. According to Dr. Sally Satel, "Pre-market review is commonly used to prove that very risky products, like drugs, medical devices, pesticides and aircraft engines, aren't harmful."[70] The premarket approval process for tobacco products was designed to protect the public from known carcinogens—tobacco cigarettes. It requires that ESD manufacturers go through an extremely expensive process that takes on average more than five thousand hours and costs from $300,000 to $2 million per product or e-liquid flavor. Satel writes in the *New York Times*, "Only the large tobacco producers would be able to shoulder these costs. . . . This would suppress the innovation that's crucial to expanding, refining and enhancing the safety and appeal of e-cigarettes."[71] In other words, the quality of ESDs would decrease, making them less appealing to smokers.

Small and medium-sized ESD businesses are understandably concerned about what a premarket review requirement would do to the industry. Gregory Conley, president of the American Vaping Association, says, "As proposed, the FDA's regulation would decimate nearly every single small and medium-sized business in this market. Thousands of businesses would close overnight. And nearly the entire e-cigarette market would become either big tobacco or firms that are backed heavily by Wall Street money."[72] Even the FDA has agreed this is the case; in its own analysis, it states that costs of premarket review "would be high enough to expect additional product exit, consolidation, and reduction in variety compared with the baseline."[73] In other words, the financial burden of having to comply with unnecessarily rigorous regulations, not the inability to prove a product's safety, is what would drive nearly all but the biggest ESD manufacturers out of the industry.

Profit, Not Health Concerns, Are Driving Regulation

Because big tobacco companies would profit from strict regulation of ESDs, they are one of the main supporters of these regulations. In a 2015 article published in *Regulation* magazine titled "Bootleggers, Baptists, and E-cigs," the authors make the argument that the tobacco companies support expensive regulation because they know it will eliminate the competition. The title of the article comes from the Prohibition laws of the 1920s and 1930s, when bootleggers—makers of illegal alcohol products—supported laws prohibiting alcohol sales because it eliminated their competition—those who made alcohol legally. Tough regulation on ESDs would accomplish the same thing, reducing competition from small manufacturers for tobacco companies.

Big tobacco companies are not the only ones that will benefit financially from ESD regulation. As more and more people embrace ESDs as a way to quit smoking or reduce their tobacco consumption, the pharmaceutical companies that make nicotine patches, gum, and antismoking medications like Chantix lose money. States also benefit from restrictions on ESDs. According to political commentator George Will, "States addicted to tobacco taxes need a large and renewable supply of smokers, so they wince whenever an e-cigarette displaces a traditional cigarette." Will explains that both government and pharmaceutical companies "are now bootleggers masquerading as Baptists,"[74] claiming to oppose ESDs for health reasons when they actually are opposing them for financial reasons.

All three of these entities—big tobacco companies, the pharmaceutical lobby, and government—are involved in ESD research and can manipulate the way study results are presented to the public and to governmental review panels. This is one reason there is so much junk science (studies that do not adhere to scientific standards of proof), misinformation, and alarmism reported in the media—those who stand to profit from regulation are spinning the facts in their favor.

ESDs have the potential to save countless lives that otherwise would be lost to cigarette smoking. Regulations that attempt to equate ESDs with deadly tobacco products will discourage smokers from quitting with the help of ESDs and will benefit those who make money from the tobacco industry.

Source Notes

Overview: E-cigarettes and Vaping

1. Quoted in Brady Dennis, "High School, Middle School Kids Now Use More E-cigs than Tobacco: CDC," *Washington Post*, April 16, 2015. www.washingtonpost.com.
2. Dina Fine Maron, "Smoke Screen: Are E-cigarettes Safe?," *Scientific American*, May 1, 2014. www.scientificamerican.com.
3. Quoted in Jeff Wagner, "E-cigarette Users, Shop Owners Prepared for Regulation," WISHTV, January 2, 2015. http://wishtv.com.

Chapter One: Are E-cigarettes and Vaping a Health Hazard?

4. Quoted in Jenny Lei Bolario, "Candy Flavors Put E-cigarettes on Kids' Menu," NPR, February 17, 2014. www.npr.org.
5. Dow Chemical Company, "Product Safety Assessment, DOW Propylene Glycol," October 3, 2013. http://msdssearch.dow.com.
6. Menfil Orellana-Barrios et al., "Electronic Cigarettes—a Narrative Review for Clinicians," *American Journal of Medicine*, July 2015, p. 679.
7. Quoted in NBC News, "Before You Vape: High Levels of Formaldehyde Hidden in E-cigs," January 21, 2015. www.nbcnews.com.
8. Quoted in NBC News, "Before You Vape."
9. Quoted in Dennis Thompson, "E-cigarette Vapor's Potentially Harmful Particles," WebMD, May 7, 2014. www.webmd.com.
10. Quoted in Anna Edney, "Is Smoking Cherry E-cigarettes Riskier than Eating Cherry Candy?," BloombergBusiness, April 15, 2015. www.bloomberg.com.
11. Peyton Tierney et al., "Flavour Chemicals in Electronic Cigarette Fluid," *Tobacco Control*, April 15, 2015. http://tobaccocontrol.bmj.com.
12. Quoted in Carol Pearson, "Report: E-cigarettes Can Cause Permanent Brain Damage for Teens," Voice of America, April 30, 2015. www.voanews.com.

13. Quoted in *Addiction*, "New Study Challenges Claims on Aldehyde Content of Third Generation E-cigarettes," August 2015. www .addictionjournal.org.

14. American Lung Association, "Smoking," 2015. www.lung.org.

15. Quoted in *Addiction*, "WHO-Commissioned Report on E-cigarettes Misleading, Say Experts," September 2014. www.addictionjour nal.org.

16. Michael Siegel, "Data from 2014 UK Youth Survey Show No Non-smoking Youths Becoming Regular E-cigarette Users," *The Rest of the Story: Tobacco News Analysis and Commentary* (blog), July 28, 2015. http://tobaccoanalysis.blogspot.com.

17. Linda Bauld, "There's No Evidence E-cigarettes Are as Harmful as Smoking," *Guardian* (Manchester), February 23, 2015. www.the guardian.com.

18. Quoted in Matt McConnell, "E-cigarette Brands Face Proposed FDA Regulations," Electronic Cigarette Consumer Reviews, April 25, 2014. www.electroniccigaretteconsumerreviews.com.

19. Tom Pruen, "E-cigarettes Are Just as Addictive as the Real Thing, Press Release Says," Electronic Cigarette Industry Trade Association, July 27, 2015. http://ecita.org.uk.

20. Joel Nitzkin, Konstantinos Farsalinos, and Michael Siegel, "More on Hidden Formaldehyde in E-cigarette Aerosols," *New England Journal of Medicine*, April 16, 2015. www.nejm.org.

21. Joe Nocera, "Is Vaping Worse than Smoking?," *New York Times*, January 27, 2015. www.nytimes.com.

22. Quoted in Lindsay Fox, "New Study Looks at the Long-Term Behavior of Vapers and Dual Users," EcigaretteReviewed, November 12, 2013. http://ecigarettereviewed.com.

23. Dan Hurley, "Nicotine, the Wonder Drug?," *Discover*, February 5, 2014. www.discovermagazine.com.

Chapter Two: Does the E-cigarette Industry Target Minors?

24. Matthew Myers, "E-cigarette Firms Are Behaving More and More like Cigarette Companies—FDA Regulation Urgently Needed," Campaign for Tobacco-Free Kids, November 5, 2013. www.tobac cofreekids.org.

25. Randye Hoder, "E-cigarette Marketers Have an Eye on Teens," *Motherlode* (blog), *New York Times*, September 6, 2013. http://parenting.blogs.nytimes.com.

26. Campaign for Tobacco-Free Kids, "7 Ways E-cigarette Companies Are Copying Big Tobacco's Playbook," October 2, 2013. www.tobaccofreekids.org.

27. Quoted in Debbie Elliott, "E-cigarette Critics Worry New Ads Will Make 'Vaping' Cool for Kids," NPR, March 3, 2014. www.npr.org.

28. Quoted in Alan Mozes, "E-cigarette Advertising Soars on American TV, Study Finds," HealthDay, June 2, 2014. http://consumer.healthday.com.

29. Ron Chapman, "State Health Officer's Report on E-cigarettes: A Community Health Threat," California Department of Public Health, January 2015. www.cdph.ca.gov.

30. David Kessler and Matthew Myers, "It's Time to Regulate E-cigarettes," *New York Times*, April 23, 2015. www.nytimes.com.

31. Quoted in Youth Radio, "Do Vape Pens Trick Teens?," video, December 2, 2013. www.youtube.com.

32. Quoted in Bolario, "Candy Flavors Put E-cigarettes on Kids' Menu."

33. Quoted in Bolario, "Candy Flavors Put E-cigarettes on Kids' Menu."

34. Mike Floorwalker, "10 Facts That Everyone Gets Wrong About Vaping," Listverse, November 12, 2014. http://listverse.com.

35. Quoted in Bolario, "Candy Flavors Put E-cigarettes on Kids' Menu."

36. Quoted in Bolario, "Candy Flavors Put E-cigarettes on Kids' Menu."

37. Jenny McCarthy, "Blu Electronic Cigarettes—Jenny McCartney [sic]—New Rechargeable Pack," YouTube, May 9, 2014. www.youtube.com.

38. Quoted in Consumer Advocates for Smoke-Free Alternatives Association, "8 Biggest Electronic Cigarette Myths." http://casaa.org.

39. Floorwalker, "10 Facts That Everyone Gets Wrong About Vaping."

40. Quoted in Heather Walker, "Target 8 Undercover: Kids Buy E-cigs," WoodTV.com, February 5, 2015. http://woodtv.com.

41. Floorwalker, "10 Facts That Everyone Gets Wrong About Vaping."

42. John Madden, "Electronic Cigarette Flavors Are Not Targeted at Minors." EcigaretteReviewed, September 25, 2013. http://ecigarettereviewed.com.

43. Consumer Advocates for Smoke-Free Alternatives Association, "8 Biggest Electronic Cigarette Myths."

44. Konstantinos Farsalinos et al., "Impact of Flavour Variability on Electronic Cigarette Use Experience: An Internet Survey," *Journal of Environmental Research and Public Health*, December 17, 2013. www.ncbi.nlm.nih.gov.

45. Madden, "Electronic Cigarette Flavors Are Not Targeted at Minors."

46. Quoted in Bolario, "Candy Flavors Put E-cigarettes on Kids' Menu."

Chapter Three: Are E-cigarettes and Vaping a Gateway to Tobacco Products?

47. Chapman, "State Health Officer's Report on E-cigarettes."

48. Quoted in Rob Stein, "Teens Now Reach for E-cigarettes over Regular Ones," NPR, December 16, 2014. www.npr.org.

49. Quoted in Youth Radio, "Do Vape Pens Trick Teens?"

50. Amy Fairchild et al., "The Renormalization of Smoking? E-cigarettes and the Tobacco 'Endgame,'" *New England Journal of Medicine*, January 23, 2014. www.nejm.org.

51. Claire Micks, "E-cigarettes—Is 'Vaping' in Front of Our Children Socially Acceptable?," TheJournal.ie, May 17, 2014. www.thejournal.ie.

52. Quoted in Daniel Cressey, "E-cigarettes: The Lingering Questions," *Nature*, August 26, 2014. www.nature.com.

53. Quoted in Cameron Scott, "Worst Fears About Teen E-cigarette Use Justified, New Data Suggest," Healthline News, December 15, 2014. www.healthline.com.

54. Quoted in Scott, "Worst Fears About Teen E-cigarette Use Justified, New Data Suggest."

55. Quoted in Martinne Geller, "E-cigarette Use Rare in Non-smokers, UK Survey Finds," Reuters, December 10, 2014. www.reuters.com.

56. Quoted in Cressey, "E-cigarettes."

57. Quoted in Kenny Spotz, "New Research Considers: Does Vaping Lead to Smoking?," *Mt. Baker Vapor* (blog), July 2, 2015. http://blog.mtbakervapor.com.

58. Quoted in Brenda Goodman, "E-cigarettes May Not Be Gateway to Smoking: Study," HealthDay, October 29, 2013. http://consumer.healthday.com.

59. Quoted in Valeo, "Study Finds Nicotine Safe, Helps in Alzheimer's, Parkinson's."

60. Quoted in Valeo, "Study Finds Nicotine Safe, Helps in Alzheimer's, Parkinson's."

61. Quoted in Michael Blanding and Madeline Drexler, "The E-cig Quandary," Harvard T.H. Chan School of Public Health, May 5, 2015. www.hsph.harvard.edu.

Chapter Four: How Should E-cigarettes and Vaping Be Regulated?

62. Floorwalker, "10 Facts That Everyone Gets Wrong About Vaping."

63. Quoted in Matt Richtel, "Selling a Poison by the Barrel: Liquid Nicotine for E-cigarettes," New York Times, March 23, 2014. www.nytimes.com.

64. Quoted in Richtel, "Selling a Poison by the Barrel."

65. Tyler McCanus, "Alert! False E-liquid Nicotine Levels at Vape Shops," Electronic Cigarette Consumer Reviews, February 2, 2015. www.electroniccigaretteconsumerreviews.com.

66. Quoted in Geoff Williams, "E-cigarette Retailers Welcome and Worry About Proposed Indiana Regulations," Al Jazeera America, April 30, 2015. http://america.aljazeera.com.

67. Quoted in Williams, "E-cigarette Retailers Welcome and Worry About Proposed Indiana Regulations."

68. Jon Deak, "It's About Damn Time We Told the Truth About E-cigarettes!," Electronic Cigarette Consumer Reviews, January 29, 2015. www.electroniccigaretteconsumerreviews.com.

69. Quoted in American Vaping Association, "Anti-smoking Advocates Urge Rejection of PA Vaping Ban," June 15, 2015. http://vaping.info.

70. Sally Satel, "Will the FDA Kill Off E-cigs?," New York Times, January 18, 2015. www.nytimes.com.

71. Satel, "Will the FDA Kill Off E-cigs?"

72. American Vaping Association, "FDA E-cig Regulations Would 'Decimate' Small Businesses," December 13, 2014. http://vaping.info.

73. Quoted in Sally Satel and Alan Viard, "A Flawed E-cigarette Regulation," American Enterprise Institute, August 16, 2014. www.aei.org.

74. George Will, "In the Crusade Against E-cigs, Government Is Hardly a Disinterested Party," *National Review*, April 22, 2015. www.nationalreview.com.

E-cigarette and Vaping Facts

History

- In 1963 Herbert Gilbert was the first person to patent a "smokeless tobacco cigarette." It was never produced.
- The modern ESD was invented by Chinese chemist Hon Lik in 2000.
- The first e-cigarette came on the market in China in 2004 and in the United States in 2007.
- In 2009 the FDA attempted to ban e-cigarette shipments into the United States. It was successfully sued by the e-cigarette industry.

Industry Facts

- In 2014 market analysts at Wells Fargo estimated that there were eighty-five hundred brick-and-mortar vape shops in the United States.
- Wells Fargo also said that in 2015 the ESD industry was estimated to be worth $3.5 billion; $1.2 billion of that total is generated by vape shops.
- According to *USA Today*, there are currently more than 460 brands of ESDs on the market.
- The antismoking group Legacy found that in 2013, blu, which is owned by a tobacco company, spent more money on advertising than all other brands combined, accounting for 56 percent of all ESD ad spending.

Prevalence

- According to the National Youth Tobacco Survey, from 2011 to 2014 ESD use among high school students increased nearly 800 percent.

- A 2014 survey by Legacy found that 39 percent of young adults ages eighteen to twenty-one had tried e-cigarettes, and 29 percent reported current use, including 65 percent of current smokers.

- The Health Information National Trends Survey found that national awareness of ESDs went from 16.4 percent in 2009 to 77.1 percent in 2013.

- The Campaign for Tobacco-Free Kids reports that the number of adolescents who have used e-cigarettes but have never smoked a tobacco cigarette more than tripled between 2011 and 2013. These children are nearly twice as likely to say that they intend to smoke regular cigarettes in the future.

E-cigarettes Versus Tobacco Cigarettes

- According to the American Lung Association, 80 percent to 90 percent of all lung cancer deaths are caused by smoking tobacco. As of 2015 no instances of cancer have been linked to ESDs.

- According to the American Lung Association, statistics from 2013 show that 76.8 percent of people who recently used ESDs also currently smoke tobacco cigarettes.

- According to Bill Godshall, executive director of Smokefree Pennsylvania, as of 2015 ESDs had replaced a total of about 2 billion packs of cigarettes in the United States.

- The American Association of Public Health Physicians Tobacco Control Task Force estimates that a national harm-reduction initiative that emphasized ESDs could save the lives of 4 million of the 8 million adult smokers in the United States who will die of a tobacco-related illness over the next twenty years.

Safety

- The American Lung Association notes that ESD vapor has been found to contain small amounts of nitrosamines, one of the main cancer-causing substances in tobacco.

- According to the American Association of Public Health Physicians, ESDs produce about the same level of trace contaminants as FDA-approved nicotine-replacement-therapy products.
- A 2014 study published in *BMC Public Health* found no evidence that the amounts of chemicals in secondhand vapor pose any risk to bystanders.
- A 2015 study at Johns Hopkins University found that mice exposed to ESD vapor were more likely to contract influenza and pneumonia.

Related Organizations and Websites

American Lung Association
55 W. Wacker Dr., Suite 1150
Chicago, IL 60601
phone: (800) 586-4872 • e-mail: info@lung.org
website: www.lung.org

The American Lung Association is a health organization dedicated to saving lives by improving lung health and preventing lung disease through education, advocacy, and research. The association is currently is fighting for increased ESD regulation. Its website contains information and research about the effects of ESDs and vaping.

American Vaping Association (AVA)
736 Washington St.
Hoboken, NJ 07030
phone: (609) 947-8059
website: www.vaping.info

The AVA is a nonprofit organization that advocates for small businesses in the ESD industry. The association educates the public and government officials about health benefits offered by vapor products. Its website contains information about the current ESD controversy as well as links to pro-vaping resources.

California Tobacco Control Program (CTCP)
California Department of Public Health
CDIC/Tobacco Control Program
Attention: TobaccoFreeCA.com
Mail Stop 7206
PO Box 997377
Sacramento, CA 95899
website: www.tobaccofreeca.com

The CTCP's mission is to fight tobacco and ESD products in California through educational campaigns and activism. It currently runs California's Still Blowing Smoke campaign, which opposes ESD use. Its website contains resources, ads, videos, a timeline of tobacco control in California, and educational information.

Campaign for Tobacco-Free Kids
1400 Eye St. NW, Suite 1200
Washington, DC 20005
phone: (202) 296-5469 • fax: (202) 296-5427
website: www.tobaccofreekids.org

The Campaign for Tobacco-Free Kids works to reduce tobacco use and prevent kids from smoking. The organization provides information and resources about the dangers of ESDs. Its website links to its blog, *Tobacco Unfiltered*, which contains news updates, opinion pieces, and research about ESDs.

Centers for Disease Control and Prevention (CDC)
1600 Clifton Rd.
Atlanta, GA 30329
phone: (800) 232-4636
website: www.cdc.gov

The CDC is a federal agency charged with protecting public health by focusing national attention on developing and applying disease control and prevention. The CDC works through the Office on Smoking and Health to reduce the death and disease caused by tobacco use. The agency has conducted research on the safety of ESDs, which it reports on its website.

Consumer Advocates for Smoke-Free Alternatives Association (CASAA)
PO Box 652
Wilbraham, MA 01095
phone: (202) 241-9117
website: www.casaa.org

CASAA is an advocacy group dedicated to raising awareness about ESDs and vaping and protecting the rights of smokers to access reduced-harm alternatives to tobacco products. Its website contains research materials and information about ESDs.

Medical Organizations Supporting Vaping and Electronic Cigarettes (M.O.V.E.)

e-mail: efvispain.info@gmail.com

website: www.moveorganization.org

M.O.V.E., which is based in Spain, is an organization made up of medical professionals who support the use of ESDs as a reduced-harm alternative to smoking. Its website contains articles, research materials, and a list of links that support ESDs and vaping.

Tobacco Vapor Electronic Cigarette Association (TVECA)

1005 Union Center Dr., Suite F

Alpharetta, GA 30004

phone: (888) 998-8322

e-mail: info@tveca.com

website: www.tveca.com

The TVECA is an international trade association dedicated to creating a sensible and responsible electronic cigarette market. The organization provides the media, legislative bodies, and consumers with education and research about ESDs and vaping.

For Further Research

Periodicals

Jonathan Adler et al., "Bootleggers, Baptists, and E-cigs," *Regulation*, Spring 2015, pp. 30–35.

Reuters, "U.S. Minors Easily Buy E-cigarettes Online: UNC Study," *New York Times*, March 2, 2015.

Matt Richtel, "Selling a Poison by the Barrel: Liquid Nicotine for E-cigarettes," *New York Times*, March 23, 2014, p. A1.

Sally Satel, "Why the CDC Has It Wrong About the Rise in Teen Vaping," *Forbes*, April 23, 2015.

Internet Sources

Carrie Arnold, "Vaping and Health: What Do We Know About E-cigarettes?," *Environmental Health Perspectives*, September 2014. http://ehp.niehs.nih.gov/122-a244.

Jenny Lei Bolario, "Candy Flavors Put E-cigarettes on Kids' Menu," NPR, February 17, 2014. www.npr.org/sections/health-shots/2014/02/17/276558592/candy-flavors-put-e-cigarettes-on-kids-menu.

California Department of Public Health and California Tobacco Control Program, *State Health Officer's Report on E-cigarettes: A Community Health Threat.* Sacramento, 2015. www.cdph.ca.gov/programs/tobacco/Documents/Media/State%20Health-e-cig%20report.pdf.

Centers for Disease Control and Prevention, "Tobacco Use Among Middle and High School Students—United States, 2011–2014," *Morbidity and Mortality Weekly Report*, April 17, 2015. www.cdc.gov/mmwr/preview/mmwrhtml/mm6414a3.htm.

Legacy for Health, *Vaporized: E-cigarettes, Advertising, and Youth*, 2014. http://legacyforhealth.org/content/download/4542/63436/version/1 /file/LEG-Vaporized-E-cig_Report-May2014.pdf.

Neil Mclaren, "Big Survey 2014—Initial Findings Eliquid," Vaping.com, July 17, 2014. http://vaping.com/data/big-survey-2014-initial-findings -eliquid.

Jesse Rifkin, "E-cigarettes Are Now More Popular with Young People than Regular Cigarettes," *Huffington Post*, April 16, 2015. www.huff ingtonpost.com/2015/04/16/e-cigarettes-smoking-health_n_7080548 .html.

Sally Satel and Alan Viard, "A Flawed E-cigarette Regulation," American Enterprise Institute, August 16, 2014. www.aei.org/publication/a -flawed-e-cigarette-regulation.

Index

About the Author

Christine Wilcox writes fiction and nonfiction for young adults and adults. She has worked as an editor, an instructional designer, and a writing instructor. She lives in Richmond, Virginia, with her husband, David, and her son, Doug.